ADVANCED
FLY CASTING

ADVANCED FLY CASTING

*For Greater Distance and
More Effective Fishing*

LEFTY KREH

Preface by Les Adams

THE LYONS PRESS

Guilford, Connecticut
An imprint of The Globe Pequot Press

The Lyons Press is an imprint of The Globe Pequot Press.

Cover photograph by Lefty Kreh.

Color photography by Andy Anderson (page 14), R. Balentine Atkinson/Frontiers (pages 44/45, 90/91), Lefty Kreh (pages 2, 11, 70, 136/137, 152/153), Tom Montgomery (pages 20, 64/65, 116/117).

FRONTISPIECE: *Lefty Kreh executes a cast.*

Printed in the United States of America

10 9 8 7 6 5 4 3 2 1

Library of Congress Cataloging-in-Publication Data is available on file.

CONTENTS

PUBLISHER'S PREFACE

In reviewing the material that Lefty was sending us for this book, I began to realize that for most of our readers, this might very well be the most valuable book in the entire series, and worth a special word or two.

To explain why I think this book is so important, let me go back in time a little bit. Whenever Lefty and I get together to work on the Library, he coming from Baltimore, I from Birmingham, naturally we try to meet in a place near water with fish in it. So I've been a most fortunate person to have fished with Lefty a number of times. I say "fortunate" not only because I honor his friendship so much, but also because Lefty's a real hoot to be with. But there is a dark side to this tale.

Every time we get together, Lefty always checks me out on how well my casting is coming along. "All right, Les," he says, "Get up there and show me your best cast." So I'll give it my best shot. And Lefty will say, "Is that it? Is that the best that you've got? Boy, the fish are going to be smiling today!"

But I react pretty well to abuse, and during the last year or so, I have really been working on improving my casting. And with Lefty's help, I have. Which brings me to the point of this story. My improvement began on the day when I actually began not just casually to read Lefty's casting instructions, but to really concentrate on what he had to say, and then to practice on each of Lefty's casting principles — particularly the ones that were giving me trouble. In my case, over the years I had developed the bad habit of bringing my rod tip down too low on the forward cast, creating a big loop. (Amazing! Just like

Lefty said it would.) Also, I was used to making a pretty sorry speed-up-and-stop. As Lefty would say, "My speed-up wasn't so speedy. And my stop wasn't so stoppable."

As to the other elements of my casting technique, Lefty — who is the master of the left-handed compliment — once said to me, "Les, you've got a super back cast. If you could just get your forward cast organized, one day you might be able to throw a decent line." (And probably under his breath, "If you are lucky enough to live that long.")

Another thing Lefty will do is mount the casting deck of a flats' boat and deliver the entire length of the fly line at a cruising bonefish, and say to me, "Les, did you see what I was doing on that cast that you're not doing? I would reply, "Yes." Then he'd come back with, "Do you understand that? Do you understand what I'm saying?" I would reply, "Yes." Then he would say, "Well, why don't you just do it like that?" Superb athlete that he is, Lefty sometimes forgets that mere mortals, like me and you, don't have his great hand/eye coordination, his powerful forearms, his set of superior nerve endings and synapses that send messages from his brain to the muscles of his casting arm at the speed of light. When Lefty says it's easy to cast the entire fly line in an ocean breeze, it's like Ted Williams saying that hitting a fast ball coming at you at 100 mph in a night game at Fenway Park is easy. All you have to do is look at the ball and swing. Sure, Ted. And sure, Lefty.

Anyway, my point is that each of us possesses differing physiques, ages, levels of athletic ability, and perhaps, fly-casting flaws that have become ingrained in our individual techniques over the years. But I can tell you, at least based upon my personal experience with this material, that this book can be the vehicle — and I have never seen a better one — to transport you to the most advanced levels of fly casting.

Les Adams

INTRODUCTION

When I wrote the first book in the Library, *Lefty Kreh's Modern Fly Casting Method*, I intended that it would be for a diverse audience, including beginning casters, people who already had some casting experience but wanted to brush up on their fundamentals, as well as experienced fly fishermen who might not have been familiar with my five principles of modern fly casting method. You will recall that book also included a short general survey of various types of fishing casts, and of the casting errors I see being made most often. I suppose that if there were an institution named the Kreh College of Fly Fishing, that book would be the textbook for "Fly Casting 101."

Well now, folks, let's go to graduate school.

The book you are now holding in your hands is designed to introduce you to the world of advanced fly casting, which I believe can really be broken down into four areas — how to make effective casts, how to cast at greater distances, how to overcome the fly caster's two greatest enemies, wind and vertical obstructions, and most of all, how to cast *to catch fish*. That last point may sound silly, I know. After all, we are all casting to catch fish. But the problem is that so many fly casters don't know how to cast well enough to consistently catch fish — particularly the big ones, who are always the hardest!

Consider this. A hunter who can't shoot well is limited in what game he will bag. Any fly fisherman who can't cast well will find that many opportunities are lost, simply because he didn't polish his skills. I have often heard anglers say to me, sometimes rather smugly, "I'm not a very good caster, but I catch a lot of fish." My instant reply is that if that person could cast better, he or she would catch a lot more fish — and derive increased enjoyment from the sport. Indeed, one of the real pleasures of fly fishing, that doesn't exist to any degree in other kinds of fishing, is the joy of making difficult casts — even if the fish ignores your offering. Just the fact that you were able to make such a cast can bring great satisfaction.

Another of the advantages of mastering advanced casting techniques is that it will enable you to cast for long periods, either at a distance, or under tough conditions, and not tire. At this writing, I am 69 years of age. Recently, I spent two days near San Francisco, fishing with that West Coast fly-fishing legend and close friend, Dan Blanton. Using 10-weight rods, from early morning until near dark we threw lead-core shooting heads, at casting distances approaching — and sometimes even exceeding — 100 feet. But at the end of the day, I was no more tired than had I been on a day-long picnic. I am not trying to be immodest, but only to assure those who master the basics of good casting, and then polish their skills to an advanced level, that they can do the same thing every time they are on the water. When you become an advanced fly caster, you will catch more fish, more consistently, and with less effort, regardless of your age or sex.

Of course, you should spend all the time you can on the practice lawn or pond, but it's easy to fool yourself into thinking that the good casts you are able to make in a practice session can necessarily be duplicated — consistently — in a real fishing situation. For most people, most times, they cannot.

For example, I see plenty of people who in a practice session can comfortably cast, say, 40 or 50 feet, with a pretty tight loop and a decent turn-over of their fly. But get them out on the water, looking upstream at a wily old six-pound brown

Wally Vait casts on Maryland's Gunpowder Falls. ➤

trout nestled close to the bank way under some overhanging willow branches, knowing they've got to make their first cast *just right*, and that it's got to curve *just so*, and *that it's got to travel no more than two feet off the surface* to avoid getting their fly hung up, and that *it's got to land quietly* and then *drift naturally*! Or get them out on a flats' boat, with a 10-pound bonefish rapidly trucking across the bow of the boat 70 feet away, allowing them just a three-second window of opportunity to fire out a long and accurate cast! In situations like these, with their guide cussing, their palms sweating, their glasses fogging, and their bodies filling up with adrenaline, a lot of people simply blow the whole deal.

Lack of experience is a major part of their failure, of course. Of that there is simply no substitute. But lack of knowledge of advanced fly-casting techniques — the techniques that make for effective fishing — can also be a major contributor. I hope that's where this book comes in.

* * * *

Before we proceed further, I think it would be helpful to explain in layman's terms what fly casting really is. I think once this is understood, much of what we are trying to do with a rod and line will make more sense.

With plug and spin casting the lure is delivered by bending the rod (which is a flexible lever) backward, then sweeping forward with the rod bent, and then making a quick stop. When the flexed spinning or plug rod stops its forward motion, the angler releases the line. The weighted lure then *pulls* the line toward the target.

The fly rod, while generally longer, is also just a flexible lever, and before you can cast the fly, just as in plug or spin casting, you must sweep the fly rod backward to bend or load it, and then bring it forward and make a quick stop. Fly casting therefore differs only slightly from spin or plug casting.

In plug and spin casting, the weight attached to the line pulls the line forward towards the target. But with a fly rod *the line transports the fly by unrolling toward the target.*

Visualize an angler trying to cast a dry fly with a plug or spinning rod: he wouldn't be able to cast six inches, simply because with this type tackle, the practically weightless fly cannot pull the line to the target. To function properly, a plug or spinning rod must have sufficient weight — weight perhaps as heavy as that of, say, a lead sinker — on the end of the line. A fly rod needs weight, too, which is provided by the fly line. An interesting way to think of this, I believe, is to imagine that *a fly line is actually just a long, thin, unrolling sinker, and the more efficiently we can unroll that long, thin sinker toward the target, the less effort will be required.*

And once we understand that we are attempting to unroll the line in the most efficient manner, then we can better comprehend how to use casting strokes to do this.

So what creates fly line efficiency? A small or "tight" loop. Because *anytime we cause the line to unroll in a large loop we are directing much of the line's energy around a circle. But the smaller the loop, the more we cause line energy to be directed toward the target and not at a tangent to it.*

This is really the crux of fly casting — in either its simplest or most advanced applications.

Bernard "Lefty" Kreh
Hunt Valley, Maryland

CHAPTER ONE

THE FIVE PRINCIPLES OF LEFTY KREH'S MODERN FLY CASTING METHOD

Of course, advanced fly-casting techniques must be constructed upon a foundation. You'll recall that the foundation that I advocate consists of five basic principles. So before I address the advanced techniques in this book, I feel its worthwhile to briefly review my definitions of the five principles of modern fly casting and take a look at the drawings with which we illustrated them in this book.

After this brief review, I'll then turn to a discussion of how these fundamental principles can be used to create many kinds of casts to meet a variety of fishing conditions, always for more fly-fishing effectiveness, and at greater distances for those situations when greater distance is needed.

◄ *Casting to permit.*

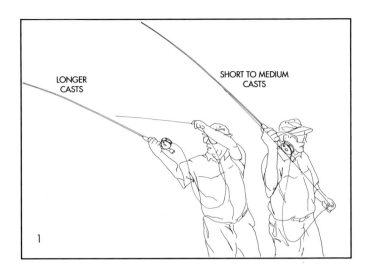

LONGER CASTS

SHORT TO MEDIUM CASTS

1

PRINCIPLE NUMBER ONE

The rod is a flexible lever which moves through varying arc lengths depending upon the casting distance required (Illustration 1).

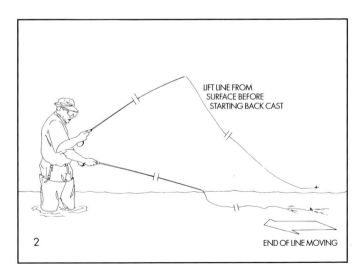

LIFT LINE FROM SURFACE BEFORE STARTING BACK CAST

2

END OF LINE MOVING

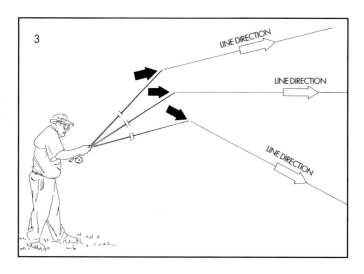

PRINCIPLE NUMBER TWO

You cannot make any good cast until you get the end of the fly line moving; and on the first back cast, the end of the fly line should be lifted from or off the surface of the water before the cast is made (Illustration 2).

PRINCIPLE NUMBER THREE

The fly line and the fly are only going to go or travel in the direction in which you accelerate and stop the rod tip at the end of the cast (Illustration 3).

PRINCIPLE NUMBER FOUR

The size of the fly line loop is determined only by the distance that you accelerate the rod tip at the end of the cast. And the faster

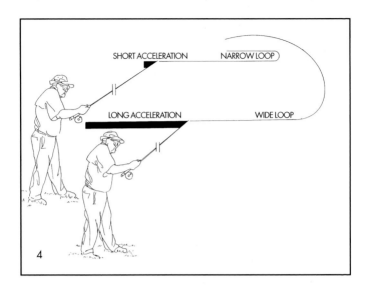

4

that you accelerate over that distance, combined with a quick stop,
the farther the cast will travel (Illustration 4).

5

PRINCIPLE NUMBER FIVE

For long or more difficult casts, you will need to bring the rod well behind your body on the back cast. In order to do this, you should rotate your casting thumb away from its normal position on top of the rod about 45 degrees away from your body before initiating the back cast, and then take your forearm (never the wrist) straight back 180 degrees from the target (Illustration 5).

OVERLEAF: *Casting to spring rainbows on Utah's Green River.*

CHAPTER TWO

ELEMENTS OF THE CAST

All fly casting is governed by the five principles set forth in the last chapter. But in addition, there are a number of other factors — let's call them "elements" — that need to be combined with the five basic principles and incorporated into your cast to achieve advanced casting proficiency. I hope I can communicate well enough to explain how to master each of these elements, but I obviously cannot cast for you. You're going to have to do some work and pay some dues to join the elite corps of advanced fly casters.

But I can assure you of this: if you are willing to take the time to carefully think through each of these elements (which as you will see I will sometimes demonstrate with both the correct and incorrect ways of doing something), incorporate them into your own casting routine, and then devote a sufficient amount of your time to practicing them, you can become a proficient advanced caster. In addition, you will have the competence to master all types of fishing situations, to make all types of advanced casts, and to make those casts with greater efficiency and at far greater distances than you were formerly capable of.

So let's get to work!

1. FOOTWORK OR STANCE

Footwork, or stance, is vital to good fly-casting technique. It assists in obtaining accuracy. But, the proper stance also permits the body to move fluidly through extended motions, which, in turn, permits the rod to travel through a long arc, aiding considerably on longer casts.

Footwork is very important in almost all sports, and certainly it is vital to good fly casting. While short casts can sometimes be made with improper footwork, longer and more difficult casts will demand detailed attention to how the feet are used. You will recall that my Principle Number One explains that the longer you move the rod through an arc the more it contributes to the cast. Proper footwork permits the body to move through longer motions, thus the rod can travel a greater distance on the back and forward casts. It also produces smooth, fluid body motions; while improper footwork restricts the body's movements and thus interferes with graceful casting.

ILLUSTRATION 6 — Here is a typical stance taken by many fly fishermen who have fished almost exclusively for trout on

6

small streams. The angler is facing forward with both feet at an even distance from the target. While this stance will work fairly well for short casts, it is very ineffective when attempting to make longer or more difficult ones.

ILLUSTRATION 7 — Because the feet remain even, the body muscles will not allow the angler to reach well back with the rod. Try this stance and you will find that your body motions are very restricted.

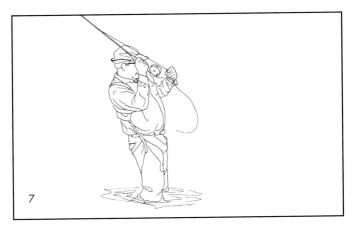

7

8

ILLUSTRATION 8 — This is the best foot position for casts other than long or difficult ones. The foot opposite the rod hand is placed about 18 inches forward of the other foot. Thus if you are right-handed, the left foot would be forward.

ILLUSTRATION 9 — When the feet are in this position, the angler can rock back and forth easily, permitting the body to flow smoothly with the cast.

ILLUSTRATION 10 — When you have to make a longer or more difficult cast, you will want to place your feet much farther apart. In fact, on a very long cast, as the rod lifts line from the surface, I will often pick up my rear foot and drop it well behind me. The main purpose of all of this is to get the rod back as far as you can before the forward cast is made, which, in turn, permits the rod to move through a much greater arc, and contributes more to making the cast. Note how the angler's weight has shifted to his rear foot, and also note the location of his hand and rod, as well as his body position at the end of the back cast!

ILLUSTRATION 11 — At the end of the back cast, the angler now faces the target with the rod almost parallel with the water.

ILLUSTRATION 12 — The rod hand is drawn forward *in a straight line*. Whatever the elevation of the rod hand at the end of the

back cast, it should stay at that elevation to complete the forward cast. The angler's weight is gradually being shifted to the front foot. If the rod hand is kept below the shoulder on a long cast, the angler can more easily attain distance.

ILLUSTRATION 13 — The weight continues to be shifted to the front foot as the rod is brought forward.

ILLUSTRATION 14 — As the line is shot toward the target almost all of the weight has now shifted to the front foot. On some long casts the rear foot of the angler will actually be lifted off the stream bottom.

2. ROD GRIP

The rod should be gripped firmly only during the speed-up-and-stop phases of the back and forward casts.

How you grip the rod is important for several reasons. A proper rod grip assists in making casts accurate and efficient, but comfort is perhaps its most important contribution. Many people get blisters when they cast. The reason for the blisters is that they are gripping the rod firmly *during all of the cast. The only time to grip the rod firmly is during the speed-up-and-stop phases of the back and forward cast.*

ILLUSTRATION 15 — The best grip, I believe, is to hold the rod as shown here, with the thumb on top and the fingers wrapped around the handle. The handle should be gripped tightly only during the last instant of the cast during the speed-up-and-stop motion.

ILLUSTRATION 16 — Here is the incorrect "index-finger-on-top" grip, one that is often favored by trout fishermen who fish

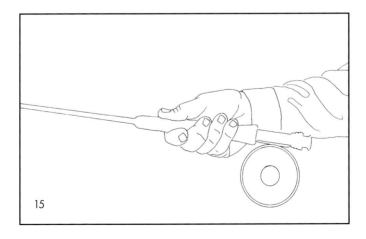

15

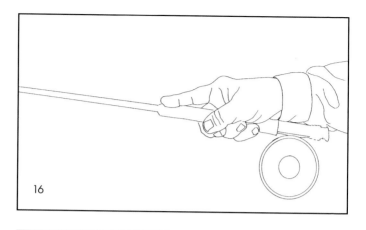

16

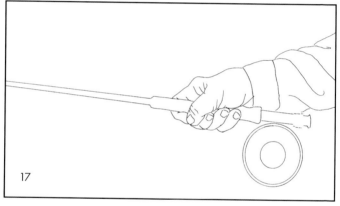

17

mainly small streams. It is a poor grip if you ever want to make longer casts, or want to fish with heavier fly rods, such as 10-weights or heavier.

ILLUSTRATION 17 — Here is yet another fairly common but incorrect grip, the "thumb-off-to-the-side" grip. This is a very inefficient way to grip a fly rod. The rod tends to roll around in the hand, and this often produces a wide, circling loop on the back cast.

3. THUMB POSITION ON THE ROD HANDLE

At the finish of back and forward casts, the thumb should be positioned behind the rod handle in relation to the direction of the desired target.

ILLUSTRATION 18 — An important point that few fly casters realize is what the position of the rod hand is *the instant after the cast ends.* This, to a large degree, will affect your accuracy. As shown in the illustration, the thumb should be behind the handle in relation to the direction of the target. Or to say it another way, the rod handle should be between the thumb and the target as the cast ends. This concept applies to both the back and forward casts.

ILLUSTRATION 19 — But if the hand turns, as shown here, so that the thumb is not on the other side of the rod handle from the target, you will find that your loops will open and some of the energy of the cast will be wasted by moving the line in a circular direction, rather than delivering all of it, most efficiently, directly at the target.

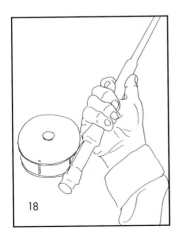

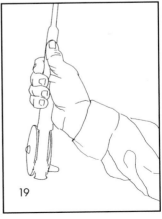

4. ROD TIP POSITION AT THE START OF THE CAST

To lift a considerable amount of line from the surface or to make a longer cast, the rod tip should be positioned well below the belt before beginning the back cast (Illustration 20).

5. ROD TIP DISTANCE ON THE BACK CAST

The distance that the rod tip travels to the rear on the back cast is dependent upon how far the angler wants to cast, or upon existing fishing conditions.

6. DIRECTION OF THE ROD TIP ON THE BACK AND FORWARD CASTS

Every back cast should travel at some upward angle (it may contact the water behind the caster if it doesn't), and, if possible, at 180 degrees or directly away from the target; and with just a few exceptions (which I will discuss later in the book), forward casts should almost always travel either straight ahead or at a slight climbing angle. That means that on most casts, the rod hand should stop in an upward direction on the back cast and should stop going either straight ahead or slightly upward on the forward cast.

Furthermore, as I have mentioned earlier, one of the most confusing things about learning to fly cast has been the improper use, by many instructors, of hour positions on a clock face to explain where to stop the rod hand.

Let me explain because this is an extremely important factor in understanding good casting technique. When making the cast, it is not *where you stop your rod hand* in reference to a clock face that is important. What is important is the *direction in which the rod tip stops.* Let's use a paper airplane to help explain this.

Holding a paper airplane between the thumb and finger, I will bring it forward three different times (as if I were making a forward cast) and each time I will stop at 10 o'clock.

ILLUSTRATION 21 — The first time, as shown, I will move my

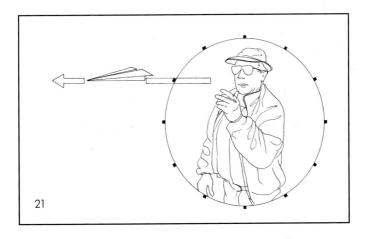

21

31

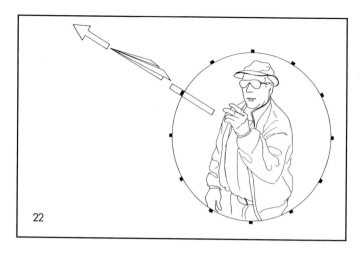

22

hand forward and go straight ahead, stopping at 10 o'clock as I release the airplane. The plane will sail straight ahead.

ILLUSTRATION 22 — The second time when I release the plane I will have my hand traveling at a climbing angle as I stop at 10 o'clock. Again, of course, the plane goes in the direction in which my hand was traveling as it stopped.

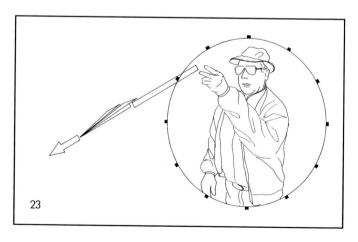

23

ILLUSTRATION 23 — On the third attempt, I will have my hand traveling downward as I stop and release the plane at 10 o'clock. Of course, the plane will crash into the ground.

What this experiment attempts to do is make the reader realize that *where* you stop on the clock face has absolutely nothing to do with where the paper plane (or the fly line) is going to travel. *It is not the position on the clock dial where you stop the rod tip that determines where the fly line will travel. Instead, it is* the direction in which you stop *that governs where the fly line will go.*

7. PUTTING ELEMENTS #1 - #6 TOGETHER: LEFTY'S CAST

The style of casting I teach greatly differs from the standard method used over the past 300 years, principally because I believe that the longer that we move the rod through a casting arc, the more the rod contributes to the cast. Therefore, I think that to execute longer or more difficult casts, on the back cast it is vital to get the rod tip well behind the angler, permitting the rod to move through a longer arc and assisting the angler in making his cast.

Many fly fishermen instinctively realize that getting the rod tip well behind them aids the cast. But more often than not, in an effort to do this they create a lot of undesirable slack in the back cast, generally in one or two ways.

In the first faulty method, from beginning to the end of the back cast, they grip the rod with their thumb up. While this thumb position is correct for short casts when the rod tip needs never to be brought beyond the vertical position, it becomes a flaw when it is maintained on the long or more difficult casts that require that the rod tip travel to a position behind the angler. With such a hand position on the rod, when these anglers attempt to move the rod tip well behind them, their forearm is naturally blocked by the anatomy of their upper arm and shoulder, resulting in the rod (and their thumb on the rod) being forced to stop at exactly or just slightly past the vertical position. When they encounter this problem, to get the rod even farther back, they break their wrists and tilt the rod back and down, so that the line is drifting, or travelling back and down. (Remember: the line is going to go in the direction in which the rod tip stops.)

I have seen some anglers who have learned to make a stop in the correct direction while letting the rod drift backwards in this manner, and who are yet still able to keep the line going up and back. However, these anglers have mastered this technique only with years of practice. But most anglers who stop their rod and then let it drift backwards will invariably place some or a good bit of slack into their back cast — slack that must be removed from the line before the rod can begin to transport the fly on the forward cast.

The other method of getting the rod back well behind the angler when the muscles of the upper arm and shoulder prevent the hand from traveling farther to the rear is to turn the rod hand outward (away from the body) in a pivoting motion. This does permit the rod to move behind the angler. But since this pivoting motion occurs just before or simultaneously with the speed-up-and-stop phase of the back cast, and since the line is going to go in the direction of that speed-up-and-stop, this outward pivoting motion of the hand will generally cause the line to unroll behind the angler in an undesirable wide horizontal loop.

This is wasting casting energy, and the fly line must be re-aligned for the forward cast.

It is vital that the line and fly travel in the exact opposite direction from the target on the back cast. What this means is that if you want the line to be 180 degrees, or exactly opposite the target, the rod hand must travel in a straight line away from the target on the back cast. And, the speed-up-and-stop must travel at some climbing angle directly away from the target. The *plane* of the cast is unimportant. That is, you could make a low side back cast and then make a vertical forward cast. But what is important is that from the start to the finish of the back cast, the rod hand should travel in a straight line away from the target.

Here is how I recommend that you do it.

ILLUSTRATION 24 — Grip the rod as you would naturally for a short cast. The thumb will be on top of the rod handle. Before you initiate the cast, *rotate the hand outward into a position for making a side cast*, as shown in the illustration. Incidentally, the farther back you want the rod to travel on the side cast, the lower the side cast should be. The higher the angle of the side cast, the less distance the rod can travel behind the angler. Therefore, when you want to move the rod as far back as possible, the side cast should be made low to the water and at only a very slight climbing angle.

ILLUSTRATION 25 — Sweep the rod hand back and at some

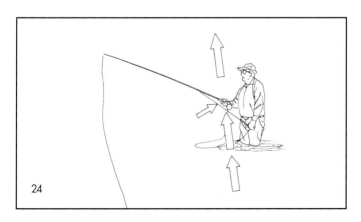

24

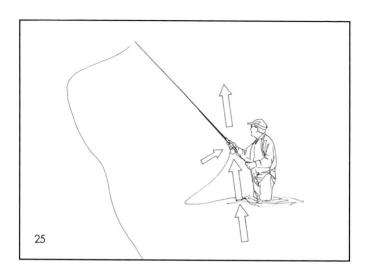

upward angle (making sure that the thumb stays behind the rod handle from the target throughout this entire motion).

ILLUSTRATION 26 — A tool that I often use to help people make a smooth straight back cast when the rod is tilted to the side,

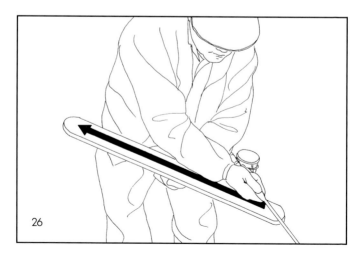

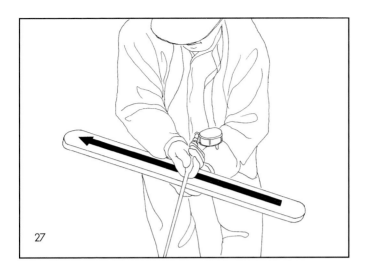

27

in the manner I have described for making longer casts, is a smooth board with an arrow taped in its center. This tool helps to emphasize that you need to make the back cast in one continuous, climbing motion — *but moving the rod hand back in a straight line.* Place the back of the rod hand flat on the board and begin to move the forearm (using only the forearm) back and up.

ILLUSTRATION 27 — The back of the hand should remain flat on the board as the hand rises and *travels straight back and away from the target.*

ILLUSTRATION 28 — If the back cast is made properly, the back of the hand will stay flat on the board and the hand, during the back cast speed-up-and-stop, will travel as the arrow indicates — straight away from the target.

ILLUSTRATION 29 — You do not want to make a side cast as you come forward. This will cause the fly to curve to the left in

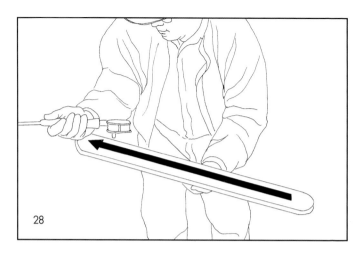

28

front of you at the end of the cast (see "Side Curve Cast" on page 126). Remember: *the line and fly are going to go in the direction in which you speed up and stop the rod tip.* Therefore, you want to make the forward cast with the rod tip traveling vertically. To perform this, at the end of the side back cast, drop the elbow slowly as the rod hand is moved forward and in toward the body to prepare for the forward cast. *It is important that at whatever elevation the rod hand was on the back cast stop, it remain at that same elevation throughout the for-*

29

30

31

ward cast. If the rod hand drops as it comes forward — which is a fault of many casters — a tailing loop may result, as I will discuss later in this chapter.

ILLUSTRATION 30 — Continue to bring the rod hand forward and in the direction of the target (making sure that you stay at the same elevation).

ILLUSTRATION 31 — A speed-up-and-stop of the rod tip in the direction of the target is made to complete the cast. During the entire back and forward cast, the rod hand has traveled in an oval — out to the side on the back cast and then brought forward in a vertical plane.

8. INCORRECT WAY TO MAKE THE BACK CAST

It is impossible for the rod tip to travel at 180 degrees away from the target when using my fly casting method if the whole arm is held straight on the back cast. The back cast should be made only with the forearm.

ILLUSTRATION 32 — If the arm is held straight when the back

32

33

cast is made, the rod hand is forced to travel in an arc or half circle, as shown.

ILLUSTRATION 33 — As shown here, since the line is going to go in the direction in which the rod tip speeds up and stops, a straight moving arm will consequently cause the line to form a large loop. Even worse, the rod tip will stop going back and to the side of the fly fisherman. Energy will now be wasted on the forward cast to get the fly line straightened and going in the direction needed. Thus a straight arm ultimately results in a very inefficient cast.

9. CORRECT WAY TO MAKE THE BACK CAST

To make the correct back cast using my method, the rod must travel exactly opposite the target (at 180 degrees); and most important, the speed-up-and-stop must also be made directly away from the target. This desirable motion can be accomplished only if the side cast is made with the forearm.

34

ILLUSTRATION 34 — The elbow is bent, and the rod will be moved rearward with the hand traveling straight away from the target. If you bend the wrist, you will spoil the cast. As shown in the illustration, the cast is made by moving the rod rearward only with the forearm and an immobile or stiff wrist. The lower the slightly upward angle of the side cast is, the farther back the rod can go. The thumb is *behind* the rod

35

handle throughout this back cast. The motion is quite similar to the action made when hitch-hiking ("thumbing" a ride).

ILLUSTRATION 35 — The rod hand continues to move straight back away from the target and at an upward angle. The speed-up-and-stop of the rod handle is made *directly away from the target*. The rod hand has traveled throughout the back cast *in a straight line*. At the end of the cast, look at your thumb. If you made a correct side back cast and did indeed travel directly away from the target you will have difficulty seeing your thumbnail. But, if you pivoted your wrist outward as you went back, or used a straight arm, you will see your thumbnail — a clear indication that you have made an improper back cast.

10. HAND ELEVATION ON THE BACK CAST

The lower the hand travels on the back cast, the less likely you are to develop casting problems on the forward cast. Ideally, on almost all casts, the rod hand should never rise as high as the caster's ear. *If the hand is kept below the shoulder, the energy of the cast is more likely to be directed toward the target, more distance can be obtained, and casting mistakes lessened.*

11. WRIST POSITION DURING THE SPEED-UP-AND-STOP PHASE OF THE FORWARD CAST

The more you bend the wrist during the speed-up-and-stop motion at the end of the forward cast, the larger will be the loop and the less efficient the cast.

The size of the loop is determined by the distance the rod speeds up and stops at the end of the forward cast. Bending the wrist will open the loop, and the more the wrist is bent, the larger the loop and the more energy will be misdirected away from the target.

This is easy to demonstrate to yourself. Without any line strung through the guides, bring your rod forward as if you are actually making a cast. When the rod is in a vertical position over your head, make a short speed-up-and-stop with your wrist immobile, using only your forearm.

Do this several times and you will note two things occurring. First, the distance the rod tip moves during that brief speed-up-and-stop motion is very short, which will always create a small, tight loop. Second — and very important — is that the rod tip is going to stop in the direction in which you want the cast to go.

Now, bring the rod to the same vertical position you did before. But this time, quite deliberately bend your wrist to make the speed-up-and-stop motion. Note that two disastrous things are occurring. First, you will readily observe that the rod tip has traveled a considerably longer distance than when you moved only your forearm, which creates a larger loop. And second, the rod will stop in a downward direction, which means not only is the loop a large one, wastefully throwing energy around a circle (with only a portion going toward the target), but some of the cast's energy is being directed uselessly down in front of you.

Of course, you'll find that there are some fishing situations when you need to create a larger loop deliberately: for example, when casting very heavy flies; or when using a very long leader, perhaps with one or more dropper flies; or when using split-shot or a large strike indicator. Throwing a tight loop for these different types of casts generally results in making a hopeless tangle of your leader.

OVERLEAF: *Casting to Atlantic salmon in Iceland.*

So, it is obviously important that you know how to throw a big loop in certain fishing situations. However, most of the time you will want to throw the most efficient loop, which will mean one that is rather small or tight.

12. HAND ELEVATION AND DIRECTION ON THE BACK AND FORWARD CASTS

A common casting mistake occurs when the hand is raised on the back cast, which causes the hand to travel in a downward direction on the forward cast. To avoid tailing loops as well as many other casting and presentation problems, the rod hand should travel directly at the target in a straight line from the beginning to the end of the cast.

A fundamental mistake made by many anglers is raising their hand on the back cast until the hand stops at an elevation even with or higher than their shoulder. It takes an accomplished caster to begin a forward cast from this high hand position and make a good presentation beyond 40 feet. In fact, I believe that stopping the hand on the back cast so that it is higher than the shoulder automatically handicaps the forward cast in several ways. First, since such consistent high back-cast stops stretch the shoulder and upper arm muscles, you will tire easily. Second, when the elevated hand and arm are carried forward to make the cast in front of the angler, the hand either has to travel in a downward direction, or worse, in a circular motion (just as the hand will travel along a circular path when a side back cast is made with a straight arm). Third, the higher the arm stops on the back cast, the more there is a tendency to throw the fly down in front of the angler, instead of out and toward the target. Fourth, a high hand-stop on the back cast results in creating one of the two most common methods of developing a tailing loop. The following illustrations demonstrate this mistake:

ILLUSTRATION 36 — Here the back cast has ended with the hand well above the shoulder.

ILLUSTRATION 37 — And now the rod hand sweeps forward as well as downward.

ILLUSTRATION 38 — The cast ends. The line and fly will go in the direction in which the rod tip speeds up and stops. Be-

cause the hand has been traveling downward, the fly line will also be traveling downward at the same angle. In addition to the problems already outlined, this often causes the line to drive into the water with a fish-frightening splash.

If, however, the rod hand is brought back low, and then carried straight forward, most of the energy of the cast will be directed at the target.

The following four illustrations demonstrate this correct technique:

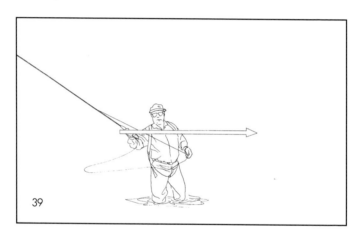

39

40

41

42

ILLUSTRATION 39 — The back cast has ended. Note that the hand is below the shoulder. It is important to understand that, when making a cast that travels parallel to the surface (as most casts do), at whatever elevation the rod hand stops on the back cast, *the hand should stay at that elevation throughout the forward cast.* I can't overemphasize this point. This factor alone will make a substantial contribution to the production of better control and longer casts.

ILLUSTRATION 40 — The angler begins to move the rod hand forward, being careful to keep the hand at the same elevation.

ILLUSTRATION 41 — The rod hand continues to move forward *in a straight line!*

ILLUSTRATION 42 — Note that the speed-up-and-stop at the end of the cast is made with the rod *still going straight ahead.* And as soon as the stop occurs, the rod is tilted slightly downward (as I will explain in further detail later in this chapter) to eliminate a tailing loop.

13. ANGLE AND ELEVATION OF THE FORWARD CAST

Most of the time, a cast should be directed at eye level. But for certain types of specialized casts, and in certain fishing situations, you will want to aim your cast at a low or high angle.

The angle at which you direct your forward cast can be an incredibly important contributor to your fishing effectiveness. Yet I am constantly finding that there exists some confusion among many fly fishermen about this subject.

Perhaps this confusion comes from their early casting instruction, as some instructors teach that you should throw the cast downward toward the target; others recommend that the cast be thrown at eye level, or parallel to the water; while others don't even deal with the subject of casting angles at all. Actually, when you think it through, there's nothing particularly complicated about this question, so it won't take me long to explain my views on casting angles.

Of course, the answer to the question is that *there really is no one correct casting angle.* You will have to experiment and decide that for yourself at streamside, based upon what you are trying to do with the cast, what kind of fly pattern and fly line you are using, where you want the fly to go, what you want to do with the line while it is in flight, what direction you want the line and fly to go, and how you expect the fish is going to react to your presentation.

The Eye Level Cast

Perhaps 90 percent of all of your casts should be directed parallel to the water's surface — or straight ahead. I often advise people to try to imagine that their target is not actually at water level, but more at their eye level, and to cast as if it really were there. While it apparently makes good sense to cast downward toward the surface of the water where the fly is ultimately going to land, there are two reasons why this may prove to be bad technique.

First, the impact of the leader, fly, and the fly line on the surface can often be disturbing enough to frighten fish.

Second, keeping in mind that the cast is going to go in the direction in which the rod tip speeds up and stops, if you want to cast, say, 50 feet, and your rod tip stops going in a downward direction, the possibility exists that the cast may actually travel a shorter distance and not reach your target; and if you perceive that happening, there's nothing you can do at this point to add more distance to your cast.

This is very much like shooting a rifle. If you aim a rifle at the ground out in front of you, that is where the bullet will strike — it certainly isn't going to go farther. But, aim the rifle at an upward angle and the bullet will travel a long, long distance. With a cast that is canted upward, as you are observing its flight path, you have the option of stopping its flight at any point along its path. Thus, to a 50-foot target, if you cast slightly upward and with enough energy for the cast to travel, say, 75 feet, when the fly is over the target simply stop its flight and the fly will fall on target. But, a cast that is directed downward will not give you this option.

I think you'll find that this eye level (or parallel-to-the-water) cast is self-explanatory.

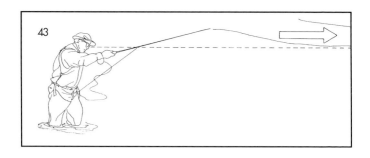

ILLUSTRATION 43 — On this cast, it's important that you make your speed-up-and-stop going straight ahead, parallel to the water, as shown, so that when the line completes its forward motion the leader will fall softly to the surface.

The Downward Cast

ILLUSTRATION 44 — Although the least used of casting angles, there are situations in which throwing the line in a downward slanting angle — directly towards the target — can be advantageous: when you want to drive the fly under overhanging brushes, boat docks, bridges, or other obstructions; or when you want to drive a streamer or popping bug under brush to attract the attention of such species as bass, snook, or redfish that are hiding underneath cover. As you know, almost all the

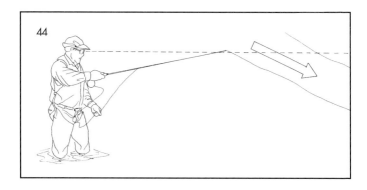

time it is good casting technique to present your fly quietly so as not to alert or alarm fish. But in these type situations, the rapid turnover and hard and loud splash-down of a fly that has been cast in a downward direction is just the ticket to bring a fish out of cover to investigate what has fallen to the water's surface.

The Climbing Cast

ILLUSTRATION 45 — In some situations, it is absolutely necessary that you direct your cast above eye level. As you will see in my discussion of individual casts later in the book, you need to use a climbing cast for *the long distance cast* — in which the upward direction of the line will help to offset the effects of gravity as the line travels out a long distance; for *the reach cast* — in which the increased height of the line above the water will allow you time to lay the rod and line over in an upstream direction; for *the tuck cast* — in which the line is high enough to allow room for the fly to sweep back under the line and fall to the surface; and for *the slack line cast* (also

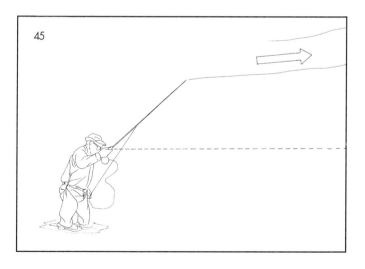

45

known by many other names, including pile cast, stack cast, stutter cast, puddle cast, etc.) — in which the dry-fly angler wants to put slack in the forward end of the line and leader to create soft "S" curves for a drag-free float.

The principal disadvantages of the climbing cast are that if it is directed *too high,* when the loop unrolls and the line is fully extended, it will fall with considerable slack in the forward end; and, of course, throwing high into a wind generally causes line to be blown back a considerable distance.

14. REDUCING THE NUMBER OF FALSE CASTS

Make as few false casts as possible. A sure indicator of a good caster is how few false casts he makes.

The advanced caster understands how to properly prepare everything before making his first back cast. This eliminates many wasted motions or mistakes that will not have to be removed by false casting during the casting sequence before making the final forward cast.

But if the advanced caster can remove faults with false casting (and many times even the very best casters can't correct a cast that simply got started badly) just the reverse is true for most people: false casts can actually create new faults that did not exist on the first cast. This is very important to keep in mind — *every false cast has the potential for going wrong:* your line hand may slip; too much slack can creep into the cast; the loop can become too open; a gust of wind can direct the line off course, etc. Thus, the more false casts that are made, the more chances are created for faults to sneak into the casting sequence.

One of the major reasons why so many fly fishermen make extra and unnecessary false casts is that they retrieve too much line from the surface of the water after their last fly presentation. Of course, you always need a certain amount of line weight outside the rod tip to properly load the rod and shoot line to the desired target. This line length can vary as a function of your individual casting skill, but no matter how well you can cast, you still need a requisite amount of line (as well as line weight) outside the rod tip. So be aware as you retrieve line *that you do not retrieve too much.* If you do, several false casts will be required to extend enough line to properly load the rod for your next cast.

A significant reason why advanced casters are able to make just a single back cast and then come forward and shoot line back to the target in one fluid back-and-forth motion is that they started their back cast with a sufficient amount of line outside the rod tip.

15. ELIMINATING SLACK IN THE CAST

If there is any slack in the back or forward cast, it will have to be eliminated with rod motion before the fly can be moved.

This principle is best demonstrated by this experiment. Place a garden hose on the lawn. Position the hose across the lawn so that there is a deep sag or single wave in it. Try to make it resemble a back cast with a deep sag. Pick up one end of the garden hose and begin walking, while looking at the other end of the hose. *You will see quickly that you won't move the far end of the hose until the entire hose straightens.*

Conduct a second experiment. Position the hose so that one end runs straight and true for a considerable distance. But at the other end form a large "U" shape with the hose, so that it resembles a back cast with a huge loop. Again, pick up the straight end of the line and begin walking. Note that the tip of the other end of the hose will not move until the large curve (representing a big fly line loop) has been removed.

The same thing applies to casting. If there is a deep sag or large loop in the line, all this slack must be removed (or the line straightened) before the rod can begin to move the fly.

16. UNDERSTANDING TAILING LOOPS

Elimination of the tailing loop from your cast is, I believe, one of the most important things you must do to become an advanced fly caster. Perhaps 99 percent of all fairly good fly casters (those who can throw 45 feet or more of line) have problems with tailing loops. And usually, the longer the cast the more likely a tailing loop will result.

A tailing loop is a cast in which, near the completion of the forward cast, the leader and/or the front portion of the line runs into the main portion of the line, creating a tangle or knot. A common explanation for this result is that a "wind knot" has developed in the leader or line (or both). *But casters get such wind knots on dead calm days. The wind has nothing to do with a tailing loop.*

Maybe why so many people fail to understand what creates tailing loops is because for years instructors have been giving their students all sorts of other explanations for the tailing loop, almost none of which really cause the problem.

For example, "shocking" the rod is supposed to cause a tailing loop. Or, applying a power stroke too soon or too late at the end of the cast is also cited. There are many other reasons that have been offered by instructors, almost all of them incorrect.

Tailing loops are caused by five distinct imperfections in *fly-casting technique* — nothing else. Before discussing these five reasons why casters tail their loops, I want to be sure you understand that *all casts are divided into two parts or motions.* First, there is the relatively long rod motion to get the line moving and the rod loaded. Second, there is the short motion of the speed-up-and-stop of the rod tip at the end of the cast.

Regarding that second motion, *it is vital to understand that the line and fly will go in the direction in which the rod tip speeds up and stops at the end of the cast! Once that is understood, it is rather easy to understand the various reasons why tailing loops are created.*

Reason #1 — Perhaps 50 percent of all tailing loops are caused by directing the rod tip straight ahead during the speed-up-and-stop phase at the end of the cast.

Remember, the line is going to go in the direction in which you speed up and stop. If you sweep the rod forward and at the end of the cast make a stop with your rod hand while going straight ahead, the tip of the rod is going to travel in the same direction, and this is going to cause the line coming from behind you to also travel in the same straight line, where it will crash into the line in front of it — a tailing loop.

Some instructors claim that if you "shock" the rod a tailing loop results. Keeping in mind that the line is going to go in the direction of the speed-up-and-stop, let's look at this explanation to demonstrate that shocking the rod is not causing the tailing loop at all. A tailing loop does occur if you sweep the rod forward and speed-up-and-stop *going straight ahead with enough force to shock the rod.* But, if you make another forceful cast and make the speed-up-and-stop motion, *but don't stop going straight ahead,* regardless of how much you shock the rod — even though this will cause the rod to dip downward slightly and likely produce numerous shock waves in the line — *there will be no tailing loop.* What caused the tailing loop was not shocking the rod, but going straight ahead on the stop.

Let me illustrate the steps involved in this common way of producing a tailing loop. Here, a fairly good caster makes a series of false casts, each one beautifully executed.

Illustration 46 — During his false casts, his hand stops near his face and no tailing loop occurs.

48

ILLUSTRATION 47 — But then, note that on the final throw, the caster's rod hand sweeps well out in front, with the hand and arm fully extended to obtain more distance (a mistake!) before the stop is made . . .

ILLUSTRATION 48 — . . . and he ends up with his final cast tailing. The same principle applies if you cast too soon. If the speed-up-and-stop is made too soon, *there is a great tendency to shove the rod hand (and rod tip) straight forward, causing the line behind to run into the line forward of it.*

Reason #2 — The second most common cause of tailing loops is changing the elevation of the hand during the forward cast, as shown in the next sequence of illustrations.

ILLUSTRATION 49 — Here note that the the caster's arm is not traveling at the same elevation during the forward stroke toward the target as it sweeps the rod forward, but begins at one elevation and drops downward as the hand is brought forward to complete the cast.

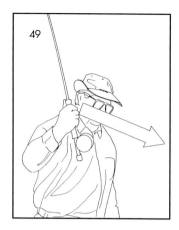

ILLUSTRATION 50 — And, anytime that the rod hand travels in a downward and forward direction like this, you are really stopping the rod tip from going in a straight line.

ILLUSTRATION 51 — And you are causing the back cast line to be pulled down on top of the portion of the line that is unrolling towards the target, like this.

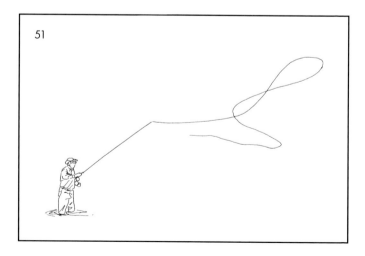

Reason #3 — While this is a relatively uncommon fault, just the reverse of Reason #2 will also cause a tailing loop. In this case the rod would begin at one elevation and then be directed to travel upwards.

ILLUSTRATION 52 — Note that if the rod hand travels from a low position. . .

ILLUSTRATION 53 — . . . and climbs upward on the forward cast, but travels in a straight line . . .

ILLUSTRATION 54 — . . . there will be a tailing loop.

I find that Reason #3 occurs much more frequently with anglers in the West than those who live in the East, perhaps because Westerners fly fish more often by wading in deep water or from a belly boat. In either of these situations, when the trunk of the angler's body is close to the surface of the water, it is necessary that he throw his back cast higher so the line doesn't hit the surface of the water behind him.

But note that a common misconception exists about this particular situation: that is, the higher you elevate the rod hand on the back cast, the higher you will keep the line off the surface behind you. That just ain't so, folks! Remember, the line is going to go in the direction in which you speed up and stop the rod tip (and rod hand). So elevating the rod hand doesn't cause you to throw a higher line. Indeed it can cause just the reverse!

And, unless you are a really excellent fly caster, *elevating the rod hand on the back cast will almost certainly result in a tailing loop.*

Reason #4 — Occasionally, a tailing loop happens when a trout fisherman who is used to casting at very short distances, and who is in the habit of stopping the rod at about 12 o'clock or the near-vertical attitude, tries to make a longer cast. When he stops his rod in a position almost straight up on the back cast, he can throw the line about 25 feet and no tailing loop will occur. But, if he attempts to throw a longer cast from this same position, a tailing loop will almost certainly occur. This is because his line has been cast straight back and then brought forward in a straight line on the same plane, and the line simply runs into itself.

Illustration 55

Reason #5 — The last fault is a low, weak back cast. This is an uncommon error, but it can result in a tailing loop, even on a short cast.

ILLUSTRATION 55 — If a back cast is made so weak that the line falls down well behind the caster . . .

ILLUSTRATION 56 — . . . and then is swept forward . . .

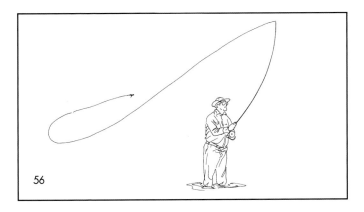

Illustration 56

OVERLEAF: *Alan Wooley fishing the Green River in Utah.*

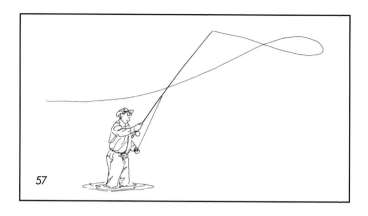

ILLUSTRATION 57 — . . . the line is in a tailing loop attitude even before the forward cast has begun.

17. CORRECTING TAILING LOOPS

Throughout this section of the book I have been stressing that stopping straight ahead at the end of the cast causes a tailing loop. But there is a paradox here. Because the line goes in the direction in which the rod tip speeds up and stops, and because we want to cast in a straight line to make an accurate cast to the target, we need to throw the line straight ahead and at the same time stop the rod tip going straight ahead. But we have learned that at this point in the cast, if nothing else occurs, we will get a tailing loop.

The key to understanding how to eliminate tailing loops is to visualize the relationship in time and space between the speed-up-and-stop of the rod tip and the unrolling characteristics of the fly line in flight.

Let's first look at the speed-up-and-stop of the rod in this way. When a rifle is fired, the moment the bullet leaves the barrel, if you threw the gun away, the bullet would still go where it was aimed. In similar fashion, as soon as the rod stops at the end of the cast, if you could magically detach your line from your rod at that moment, just like the bullet, your line would go in the direction in which the rod tip stopped. After the rod stop, *almost nothing can influence or alter the direction that the fly line and fly are going to travel!*

Next, try to visualize that when the rod stops and the line is being propelled toward the target by power of the forward cast from its position in the air behind the caster, the end of the fly line is unrolling and forming a loop which has a bottom as well as a top. The top of the loop consists of the front portion of the fly line and the leader and fly which are attached to it. The bottom of the loop consists of the balance of fly line behind the front portion. As we have already discussed, a tailing loop is one in which these bottom and top portions of the fly line (which in unrolling have formed into the configuration of a loop) crash into each other and become intermingled or tangled.

But if we can't alter the direction of the line, what are we going to do to prevent that tailing loop?

What we are going to do is *something that takes place after the speed-up-and-stop.* And we are not going to alter the direction of the fly line to do it, because, just like the bullet that has been fired, that is no longer in our power. *What we are going to do is to slightly alter the configuration of the loop,* as shown in the following sequence of illustrations:

ILLUSTRATION 58 — Speed up and stop in the direction you want the line to go (usually straight ahead) . . .

ILLUSTRATION 59 — . . . and the moment that the stop occurs, briefly tilt the rod tip downward with thumb pressure just a fraction of an inch. What happens is this. The line is directed at the target straight ahead on the stop, and if the tip is imme-

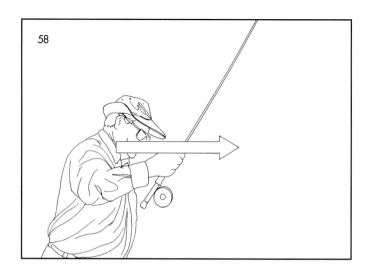

58

diately ducked or lowered a few inches a tight casting loop is maintained . . .

ILLUSTRATION 60 — . . . but without a tailing loop. By lowering the tip after the stop you have not altered the *direction* of the

59

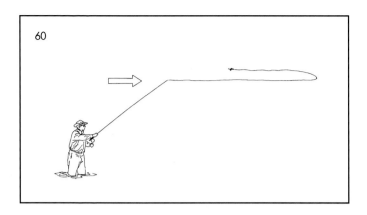

60

cast, *you have slightly altered the configuration of the loop* by insuring — with this slight and brief thumb movement after the stop — that the bottom of the loop remains on the bottom, and the top remains on top (in a tight loop configuration) so that they cannot crash into each other.

In conclusion: All your tailing loop problems will vanish if you take the following steps:

1) Make a positive back cast that will cause the line to unroll behind you.

2) Carry the rod forward in a straight line.

3) Speed up and stop the rod in the direction you want the line to travel.

4) As soon as the rod tip stops, tilt the rod tip downward very slightly with your thumb.

OVERLEAF: *Irv Swope casts to trout on Green Spring Creek, a limestone stream in south central Pennsylvania.*

CHAPTER THREE

ADVANCED CASTS FOR MORE EFFECTIVE FISHING

ROLL CASTS*

Next to the basic back and forward casts, the roll cast is the most important of all casts. Most people think that the roll cast is used only when there is little room for a proper back cast. But in various forms it can be used in every phase of fly fishing — from seeking sipping trout in a beaver pond to firing out a long shooting taper on a saltwater reef. In many fly-fishing situations, the roll cast is a versatile and marvelous tool for the advanced caster.

The five principles of casting apply to the roll cast as well as all other casts. Yet perhaps 90 percent of all fly fishermen make a faulty and inefficient roll cast, primarily because they disregard the five basic principles when they are making this

---

*The following illustrations pertain to roll casting with a floating line. Roll casting with sinking-tip or sinking lines is accomplished with the single water haul and double water haul techniques, which will be discussed later in this book.

particular cast. One of the reasons for this, I believe, has been poor instruction. I have seen one fly casting video, for example, that advocates that you should make a forward roll cast the same way that you would use a meat cleaver to chop meat. It's no wonder that most fly fishermen throw a bad roll cast! But whatever the reason, the average caster's roll cast causes the front portion of the line and leader to fall in front of him in a tangled mess.

So let's take a good look at one of these bad roll casts, as I have found that examining what people are doing wrong is frequently the best way to instruct them on good technique.

The Bad Roll Cast

ILLUSTRATION 61 — Consider the method used by almost all fly fishermen when they want to make a roll cast. The rod is brought to approximately a vertical position. As shown, the rod hand is tight against and in front of the shoulder. Most of the fly line is lying on the water in front of the angler.

ILLUSTRATION 62 — To throw the forward cast from this rod position, the angler flips the wrist of the rod hand forward and downward. And that is exactly why a poor cast results.

61

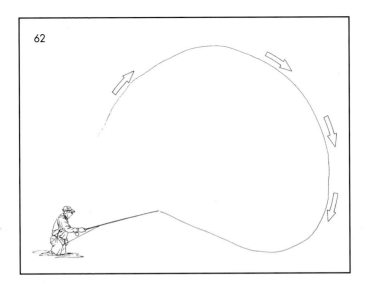

Remember the first three of the basic principles: Number One — any time you need help on a cast you need to move the rod through a longer arc; Number Two — the size of the loop is determined by the distance that the rod tip moves during the speed-up-and-stop at the end of the cast; and Number Three — the line and the fly are going to go in the direction in which the rod speeds up and stops at the end of the cast.

In Illustration 61, you can see that when the caster brings his hand back in front of his shoulder, he is really prohibiting the rod from much further participation in the cast. Then, when he bends his wrist as the rod sweeps forward, as shown in Illustration 62, he causes the rod tip to travel through a larger arc, thus producing a much larger loop which is going to throw energy around a curve instead of at the target. Finally, the rod tip on the stop is directed downward almost at his feet. This causes the line to travel in a very big loop, depositing the fly and leader in a pile in front of the angler.

The Basic Roll Cast

The first mistake that most casters make is to assume that the roll cast is made differently than other casts. *But only the back cast is executed differently.* The back cast is modified simply because in most roll casting situations you don't have room enough behind you to make a conventional cast. But, *the forward cast is made exactly like any good basic forward cast. This is the single most important point to consider when you make a roll cast.* Let me emphasize this: *on the roll cast you should not change your basic forward cast!*

Once the back cast has been properly set up, on the forward cast you should follow all the basic principles governing good fly casting: sweep the rod forward, keeping the rod hand at whatever elevation you started. Make a short, quick speed-up-and-stop, with the rod tip traveling straight ahead, and the line will unroll toward the target. For as always, the shorter the distance the rod tip travels during the speed-up-and-stop, the tighter will be the loop. And, the faster the rod tip travels during the speed-up-and-stop, the farther the line will travel.

And as always, if you want the cast to travel farther, go through the same motions, but move your rod hand (and the rod tip) faster over a shorter distance and stop quicker at the end of the cast. You do this in exactly the same way that you would if you wanted to increase distance on a conventional forward cast.

Look how simple this is getting! You know how to make a forward cast, so for the rest of this discussion we can forget about it. If the only difference between the roll cast and a conventional cast is the way a back cast is set up, that's all you need to learn! Let's do it.

ILLUSTRATION 63 — To make a good basic roll cast, set the back cast up differently in the following manner.

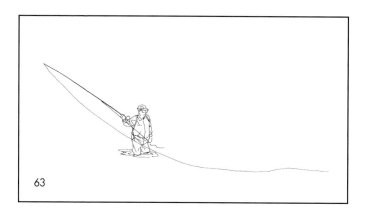

63

1) As you initiate the back cast, tilt the rod tip slightly away from you so that the line doesn't tangle in the rod during the subsequent motions.

2) Slide the line on the water s-l-o-w-l-y toward you, moving the rod tip toward the rear. *Try to keep the rod hand below the shoulder — even lower if you possibly can.* This will help you make a better forward cast. If the rod hand is held high (up to or above the ear) chances are you will automatically make a large loop — throwing part of your energy around a large curve — rather than directing it at the target area.

3) The longer you want to make the cast, the farther back you want to let the rod drift. *This illustration shows proper technique for a relatively long cast: rod hand low, arm almost straight, rod tip well back.*

4) You now need to only do one more thing to complete the back cast: *you must permit the line in front of you to come to a stop even if only for one second. This is vital to good roll casting.* The reason for the momentary stop is that you need to have some resistance for the rod to pull against when the forward cast is made, and the surface tension of the water will provide it. Surface tension *instantly* grips the line when a stop is made, no matter how briefly.

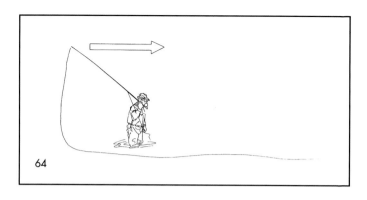

64

ILLUSTRATION 64 — After the stop, begin to move the rod forward, gradually accelerating.

ILLUSTRATION 65 — Be sure to keep the rod hand at the same elevation throughout the forward cast. Once the rod hand is in front of the body, the conventional speed-up-and-stop can be made. Make sure that the rod tip travels straight ahead.

ILLUSTRATION 66 — If the cast doesn't go as far as you like, repeat the operation, possibly taking the rod even farther back

65

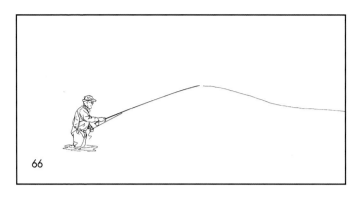

66

on the back cast and on the forward cast making the speed-up even faster and the stop more abrupt.

There are two major advantages of positioning the rod well behind you before making the back cast. Whereas with poor roll casting the rod is held in front of the angler in a vertical position with most of the line lying in front of him; with good technique, when the rod drops well behind the angler, less line has to be turned around and redirected forward. And, as the rod moves forward, it can be loaded more efficiently by the pulling force that is being exerted on the line behind him that is being gripped by surface tension.

The Tight Loop Roll Cast

This is an exceedingly useful cast, especially on trout streams. By making a tight loop that travels only a few feet above the surface, the fly fisherman can direct his line and fly underneath overhanging brush, low bridges, etc. The tight loop roll cast is generally only effective at short distances not exceeding 40 feet, but it can also add to the effectiveness of roll casts that must be made into the wind. For this cast, the height of the unrolling loop is determined by three factors: *how low you crouch, how low the rod hand is kept on the forward cast, and how brief the speed-up-and-stop is.*

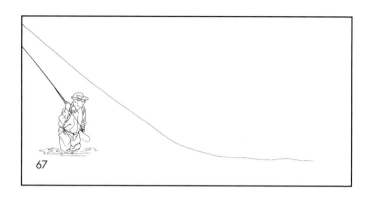

ILLUSTRATION 67 — Crouch in a low position, keeping the hand as low as possible at the end of the back cast. The closer the rod hand is to the water, the closer the loop will travel above the surface.

ILLUSTRATION 68 — Keep the hand at the elevation where it stopped on the back cast and bring it straight forward swiftly and make a conventional speed-up-and-stop. (Don't forget to tilt the thumb after the stop to eliminate a tailing loop.) The briefer the speed-up-and-stop, the smaller the loop. And the faster you speed up and stop the rod tip at the end of the cast, the faster and farther the line will unroll.

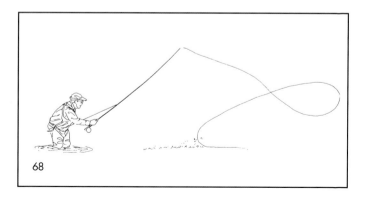

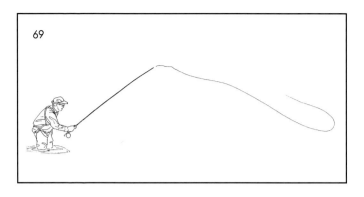

ILLUSTRATION 69 — A very tight loop will quickly unroll to the target.

The Back Hand Roll Cast

Trout fishermen, in particular, will discover that this cast is extremely useful on many occasions. A typical situation is when you are standing in the water facing upstream, tying a fly on, and the line extended outside your rod tip has drifted downstream behind you. In this situation, before you can resume casting, you are going to have to get all your line back into a proper orientation, and the back hand roll cast will save you a lot of time that can better be devoted to fishing.

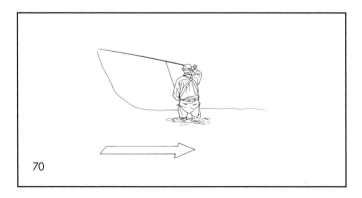

ILLUSTRATION 70 — Turn the upper body so that you are facing downstream. Slowly draw your rod up to the position shown in the illustration. This sets you up for the cast.

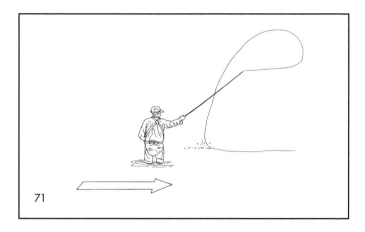

71

ILLUSTRATION 71 — Make a conventional roll cast to the rear. When the fly leaves the water, turn and face the target.

ILLUSTRATION 72 — Make a conventional forward cast and you are back to fishing!

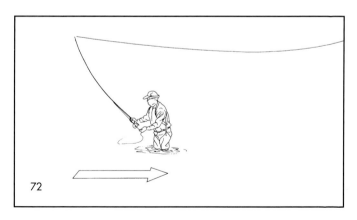

72

The Off-the-Shoulder Roll Cast

If you are a right-hander (and of course the situation would be just the opposite for a lefty) roll casting in front of you or to the left is no problem. But, when you want to direct a roll cast to your right, things get difficult. What will invariably happen is that you will tangle the line or leader on the rod. It will quickly become apparent that to make a roll cast to your right, you will need to begin the cast with the rod to the left of your body or — as it is commonly referred to — off the shoulder. But from this position, your arm and rod motions are substantially restricted, and almost no one can make as long a cast this way as he can when the rod is held in its normal position on the right of the body. Still, casts of 45 to 50 feet can be made if you follow correct technique.

However, most people make poor off-the-shoulder roll casts, principally because they start them poorly. The critical factor in this particular cast is hand and rod position at its commencement. Let's examine this incorrect technique first.

ILLUSTRATION 73 — The rod should never be drawn to the rear as shown. If the back of the hand faces the target (as shown

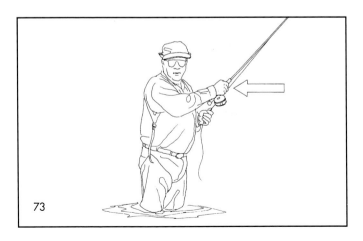

73

in Illustration 73), you will not be able to deliver a powerful sweep of the rod and efficient speed-up-and-stop motion will be impaired.

74

ILLUSTRATION 74 — From such an initial incorrect rod position, your arm can deliver only a relatively weak stroke to the ending hand position as shown.

75

ILLUSTRATION 75 — Here is the correct method. The rod is brought to the rear as shown *so that the knuckles of your hand* face the target. *From this starting hand position you can make a much more powerful arm stroke as the rod is brought forward.* And remember, as we discussed earlier, the handle should be between the thumb and the target at the end of the cast.

76

ILLUSTRATION 76 — This is the correct hand position at the end of the cast. Study the difference between this position and the incorrect one (Illustration 74).

The Side Roll Cast

Many times the angler is confronted with the problem of overhanging bushes. This is perfect cover for a fish to hide under, and since few anglers can deliver a fly or lure beneath such overhanging brush, these fish see few offerings. But the side roll cast — which is generally a fairly short cast, no longer than 35 feet or so — will permit you to deliver a fly under brush that hangs more than two feet off the water surface; often in places where hardware fishermen simply cannot throw their plugs and lures.

77

All the fundamentals of making a good roll cast apply to the side roll cast. But, you are going to change two things: 1) the plane of the cast — so that it will be parallel to the surface of the water; 2) the duration of speed-up-and-stop at the end of the cast — it must be briefer because in this situation a large, wide loop would probably tangle in the brush; whereas a very fast speed-up-and-stop will deliver a small, tight loop.

ILLUSTRATION 77 — As shown, the side roll cast is set up on the back cast just like any good basic roll cast. The rod hand is drawn well back behind the body, so that much of the line falls in a gentle curve behind the fisherman, as it would on any conventional roll cast.

ILLUSTRATION 78 — As soon as the rod stops on the backward motion, the rod tip is lowered to the side *so that the rod is parallel to the surface of the water.* It is extremely important that the rod be parallel to the surface before the forward roll cast is begun! Note that if the rod is tilted at a high angle, a bad cast will certainly result.

84

78

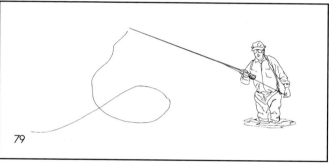

79

ILLUSTRATION 79 — The rod is swept forward *keeping it as parallel to the surface as you can make it.*

ILLUSTRATION 80 — And then, a very fast speed-up and a quick stop will cause the line to unroll parallel to the water in a tight loop toward the target.

But if the rod is tilted high above the parallel plane as the speed-up-and-stop occurs, the loop will be tilted at an angle and the fly will unroll and jump up and into the bushes. I am often successful in getting my casting students to better un-

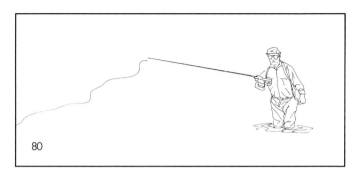

80

derstand this by emphasizing the relationship between the rod tip and the surface of the water: if the rod tip is 2 feet and 2 inches off the surface at the beginning of the speed-up-and-stop, the line will then unroll throughout the entire cast at 2 feet and 2 inches off the surface. No more, no less. Unlike very long casts, since the side roll cast is a short one, not enough time expires on this cast for gravity to pull the line down towards the surface.

The Aerial Roll Cast

The aerial roll cast is generally used only for short range work, in places where almost any other cast is impossible. It is especially useful for trout fishing on small streams in situations where a fish is spotted, but where because of backside and overhead obstructions there is neither space behind nor above the angler to make a conventional back cast or back roll cast. The aerial roll cast is effective in such a situation, but only to a distance of about 15 or 20 feet, and even less distance is better.

ILLUSTRATION 81 — Extend approximately six to 10 feet of fly line outside the rod tip. Hold the fly firmly between the thumb and the first finger. Be sure to hold the hook by the bend so that its point won't impale you. Lower the rod so that it points

81

at the target. *It is vital to begin this cast with the rod tip just inches above the water and with the tip directed at the target.*

ILLUSTRATION 82 — Sweep the rod tip swiftly up *and directly away from the target.* Maintain a firm (but not too tight) grip on the fly. How high you bring the rod tip before making the forward cast is dependent upon the height of the obstructions over your head. Ideally, if you can sweep the rod tip at least up to a vertical position, the cast is easier to make. However, a cast at least 15 feet long can be made if the rod is brought up just 45 degrees or so from the surface.

82

ILLUSTRATION 83 — The rod is brought as high as conditions will allow, keeping that grip on the hook bend of the fly.

83

ILLUSTRATION 84 — The instant the rod tip has reached its highest point, it should be swept forward *immediately*. Don't make any stop between the back and forward casts! *It is vital that the change in the direction of the rod be performed with no stop.* This keeps the line and leader in a tight loop. Up to this point in the cast, you should be holding the hook firmly enough so that it will not slip out of your fingers, creating a tension that will load the rod with the line and leader sweeping through the air. *The instant that the rod begins to sweep forward, relax your grip on the fly.* As tension is released, the tight, fast-moving leader and line will pull the fly from your grip.

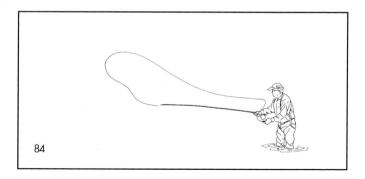

84

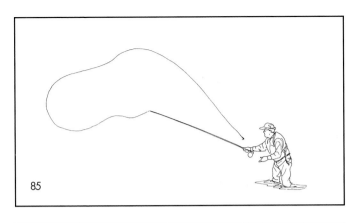

85

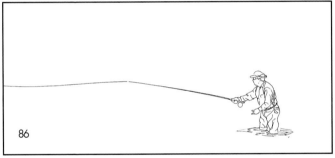

86

ILLUSTRATION 85 — On the stop, be sure to direct the rod tip in line with and well above the target. This will cause the leader and line to unroll in the air in the target's direction. If the rod tip is driven downward at the stop, the line will be thrown down and short of the target.

ILLUSTRATION 86 — After the stop, the rod can be lowered to a fishing position. If the speed-up-and-stop of the rod tip was made slightly above and in the direction of the target, the line will unroll and the fly will drop exactly where you want it.

OVERLEAF: *A first casting lesson in Iceland.*

The Roll Pick-Up

The principal value of the roll pick-up is that it permits the angler *to lift a fly vertically from the water,* and is therefore a valuable tool for many fishing situations:

1) When your dry fly is drifting on calm water and you need to lift it from the surface of the water without disturbing a suspicious trout;

2) For the line pick-up of a popping bug, in which a conventional pick-up is liable to drive the bug underneath the surface, creating a loud fish-disturbing gulping sound;

3) When retrieving a sinking line with so much line underwater that you cannot lift it for a back cast. In this situation, you need to elevate the line above the surface before the back cast is attainable. After retrieving most of the sinking line, a roll pick-up can be made that gets the line out of the water (the *single water haul* discussed on page 96);

4) When fishing underwater flies (streamers and nymphs) many times accumulated slack will make it difficult to throw a back cast. A roll pick-up will lift the line for the cast.

5) When your fly snags on a log or other obstruction, you can make a roll pick-up motion that will cause the line and leader to roll beyond the snagged fly, producing power or tension from an opposite direction to free it. The casting stroke used for this situation is identical to the roll pick-up stroke.

Master the roll pick-up and you will find you have added a powerful and useful tool to your fly-fishing technique.

ILLUSTRATION 87 — A roll pick-up follows the basic rules of the roll cast, with a few differences. Since the line is being directed *upward* and not forward as with a conventional roll cast, it will help if the rod tip is brought farther back behind you.

ILLUSTRATION 88 — Remember Principle Number Three: the line will go in the direction in which the rod tip speeds up

87

88

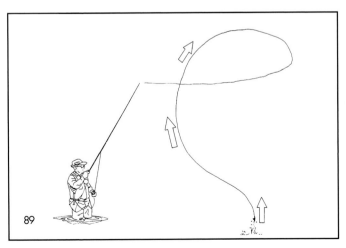

89

and stops. You want to make the cast so that the line rolls upward *and so that the front portion of the line rises almost vertically from the water!* When this occurs, the rod tip will speed up and stop as shown in the illustration — at a forward and upward angle.

ILLUSTRATION 89 — As the rod stops, the line will unroll in a loop in front of the angler. Note the fly is being pulled up and free of the water.

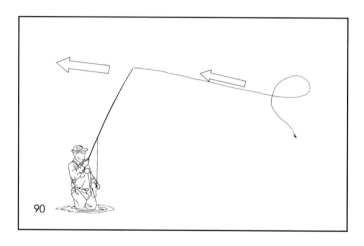

ILLUSTRATION 90 — During the cast the angler should be looking at the fly. *The moment the fly exits from the water, make a conventional back cast!*

A Special Roll Cast Variation for Removing Debris from the Fly

ILLUSTRATION 91 — If you determine there is grass or debris on your fly, it is not necessary to bring the fly to you. Instead, with a special roll cast, most of the time you can quickly eliminate the material from the hook and continue to fish. As shown, make an easy or weak roll cast that will lift just the

91

line, but not the leader and fly, from the water. What you want to do is to get the line in a roll cast *attitude*.

ILLUSTRATION 92 — Timing is critical on this cast if you want to be successful. *Watch the front end of the line, and when only the leader and fly are still on or in the water, make a hard, violent back cast! It also helps to make a haul to gain even more force or speed.*

92

The key to getting rid of the grass is to have all of the line in the air, and when you make the back cast, since the fly is still in the water, water tension will grip the grass adhering to it and press it against the hook, which acts almost like a knife blade to shear through the grass. If you have timed it properly, the fly will leap from the water free of the debris and will travel backwards. All you need to do is make your forward cast and you are back to fishing.

The Single Water Haul

Whenever you are using a fly line that is designed so that any portion of it sinks below the surface, you need to modify your roll-casting technique. The forward cast is still made the same way as a normal forward cast. But because the line is below the surface, the angler must get the sinking line out of the water before the back cast can be made.

Many people retrieve enough line so that they can lift the sink-tip or sinking line up and out of the water with a high roll cast. Then while the line is unrolling in the air in front of them, they make their back cast. This does work, but when you make the back cast in this manner, you are pulling against nothing more than air so that the rod doesn't load very well.

A much better way of roll casting any sinking line is to modify it with the *single water haul*. But to make this modifi-

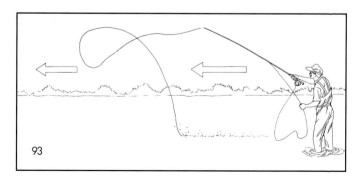

93

cation, you will need some room behind you. Here's the way to make the single water haul.

ILLUSTRATION 93 — Strip in enough line so that you can pick it up and make a roll cast which is *directed straight ahead in front of you*. This will cause the line to be driven in the direction shown by the arrow.

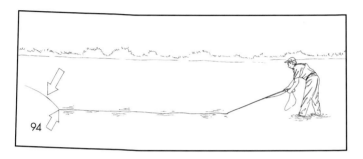

94

ILLUSTRATION 94 — The line will travel in the direction that the rod tip speeds up and stops. When the rod tip stops, lower it until it is very close to the surface.

Watch the end of your fly line. When it unrolls and the front end of the line touches the water, you are ready to make the back cast. Don't delay, or the sinking line may sink too deeply. If you begin the back cast just as the front end of the line touches down to the surface, while you have a little of the line below the surface, you can still easily lift it.

When making the back cast, you will be in the position of leaning forward with your rod tip and pointing at the fly. Make a long drawing-back motion with the rod. This long motion will allow you to load the rod better.

ILLUSTRATION 95 — When you feel that you have properly loaded the rod, make a normal back cast. You'll be amazed at how much better the back cast is than using the conventional

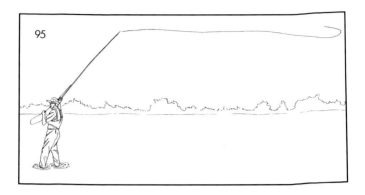

95

method of rolling the line up in the air. Then when ready, make your forward cast.

The Double Water Haul

With a sinking line, the single water haul is a great way to improve your ability to cast a long line with ease. But if you have water behind you (if you are wading or are in a boat), then the *double water haul* makes the cast even easier. This cast works especially well with sinking shooting tapers, including lead-core shooting-taper configurations.

ILLUSTRATION 96 — Bring the line up and make a roll cast so that the line straightens on the surface (just as you would when making the single water haul).

ILLUSTRATION 97 — Be sure to direct the line straight ahead and allow it to fall to the surface, just as you would with the single water haul.

ILLUSTRATION 98 — As soon as the front end of the line touches the water, make a soft or easy back cast. Make it only hard enough so that the line will straighten behind you as it falls. *Don't make a normal hard back cast!*

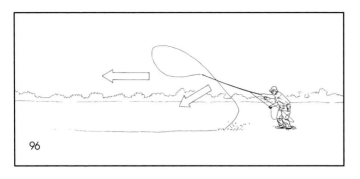

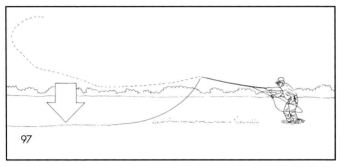

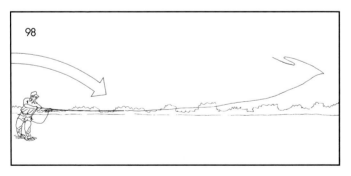

ILLUSTRATION 99 — Watch the end of the sinking line as it un-rolls and begins falling. As soon as the end of the line touches down on the surface of the water, you are ready to make the forward cast.

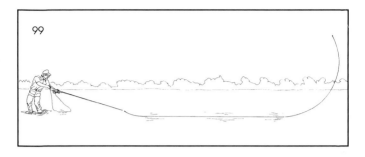

ILLUSTRATION 100 — The forward cast is made a little bit differently than a normal forward cast. As soon as the front end of the line touches the surface, begin a long drawing-back motion. When you feel that the rod is properly loaded, make a forward cast. Be sure to direct the forward cast at a high angle, as in the illustration. This high forward angle improves your ability to throw a long forward cast, and it causes the fly to travel high above your head. Anyone who has used lead-core shooting tapers or heavy flies carrying sharp-pointed hooks knows that it is better to have the fly traveling high overhead!

Use of the double water haul will allow even older people who do not possess great forearm strength to make casts with sinking shooting tapers that exceed 100 feet. And there is as little effort involved in this cast as throwing a line 40 feet!

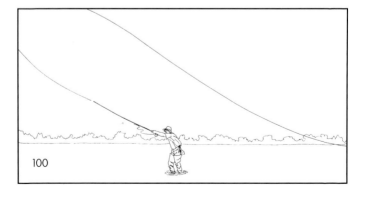

THE REACH CAST

When you need to cast across a current in the stream, you need to use a reach cast that will counteract the effects of the current on the fly line, without which a belly will be created that places unnatural drag on the fly. The reach cast permits you to place all of the line, from the rod tip to leader, upcurrent of the place where the fly has landed. This will buy you a short period of time when there will be no belly in the line, and the fly can drift downstream naturally, without line drag. It is a cast that is vital to good trout fishing, and it is also useful for fishing to other species.

There are three important factors in making the forward cast for a good reach cast. Violate any of the three components and the cast will be a poor one. 1) You must direct the cast well above your head; 2) You must make a slow speed cast; and 3) You must feed slack line from the rod as the reach is made. The following sequence of four illustrations demonstrates this cast.

ILLUSTRATION 101 — Make a conventional back cast, but try to direct the line a little lower behind you than normal. Bring the rod forward *vertically* and try to make a *slow, high cast.*

101

You will see that two of the three key factors in making a reach cast are already at play here: *you want to make the cast travel slowly enough* so that you will have time to make the reach cast; and *the cast must be high enough* to permit you to lay the line upcurrent of the fly.

If you make the cast travel too fast it will be over the target before you have the proper amount of time to move the line upstream. And, if you direct the line at a downward angle, most of the line will fall into the water before you have had an opportunity to lay it upstream on the reach.

ILLUSTRATION 102 — As soon as the rod stops on the forward cast, you need to do two things at the same time. Point the rod upstream as you lower it toward the water, reaching outward with the rod pointing upcurrent, and at the same time, permit loose line on the water to flow through your hand. This is the third vital factor. *You must permit line to flow freely through your hand and rod guides as the rod is being drifted over and upstream.* What you are doing is placing a lot of slack line upstream. If you instead hold the line in your hand while you drop the rod over the water, the slack will be created on the other end of the line, causing the fly and leader to be pulled

102

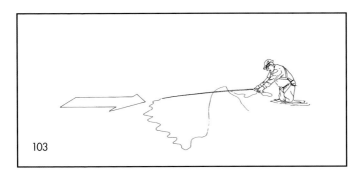

103

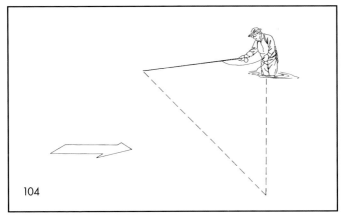

104

back, producing a poor cast. This is the major mistake most people make on the reach cast — they don't permit slack line to flow through their hand and rod guides as the rod and line are being positioned upstream.

ILLUSTRATION 103 — This illustration demonstrates how the fly line should come to the water. Note that the rod is pointed well upstream.

ILLUSTRATION 104 — As the cast ends, you will see that the line lies upstream, forming a triangle with you and the target.

THE BACK-FORWARD CAST

There are many times where a forward cast thrown to the rear, followed by a conventional forward cast in front of you, serves the fisherman better than a standard back and forward cast. What you are actually doing with this technique is positioning yourself to throw two forward casts. And I observe that most people find it easier to throw forward casts than back casts. This is primarily because very few fly casters ever bother to study their back casts. When they are facing towards the target on their forward cast, they always closely observe their forward casts, and consequently throw a much better loop and line in front of them than they do on their unsighted back casts.

Let's take a look at a typical fishing situation. Let's assume there are thick brush and trees behind you, but as you turn around and examine these obstacles, you see an opening in the brush large enough for a cast and its loop. If you were fishing (and facing) in that direction, you could likely deliver a forward cast into the opening and avoid a snag on the brush. But you are fishing in the opposite direction, and have to deliver a conventional back cast into that hole, which is difficult to do because it is unsighted. And to see better, if you turn your body on the back cast to look at the target, this body turn may contribute to a poorly directed cast.

So in this situation, how are we going to get the necessary accuracy and place our line into that opening on the back cast? We're going to get it by throwing *two forward casts*.

Another excellent use for the back-forward cast is when you need to make an immediate back cast to a fish. For example, if you are standing in a boat fishing for bonefish or tarpon and suddenly the guide yells that you need to quickly cast behind you to an approaching fish, the back-forward cast is much more accurate than trying to make a back cast. Here is the correct technique for this cast.

ILLUSTRATION 105 — Examine the opening that you need to throw the line into. Then face forward and lower the rod until the tip touches the water. It is important that you begin this cast with a very low rod.

ILLUSTRATION 106 — For this first forward cast, raise your rod so that it is parallel to the surface, turning your body so that your weight shifts to the back foot, pivoting your forearm to bring your rod into the position shown. Note that *your hand is turned so that the thumb is behind the rod handle from the target opening.* If you don't get the thumb in this position there is a tendency to throw a poorer cast.

107

ILLUSTRATION 107 — Continue to move your hand to the rear as shown. This is one of the few casts where I recommend that the rod hand be higher than the shoulder when making the speed-up-and-stop.

ILLUSTRATION 108 — As soon as your hand is about a foot behind you, complete this first forward cast and make a speed-up-and-stop with your rod point straight ahead at the opening in the brush. *But don't make it too soon. Wait until your rod hand has passed well beyond your head.*

108

109

ILLUSTRATION 109 — Because you are facing backwards looking at the opening in the brush, you can observe your line on
its travel and know where the cast is going to be delivered. As
the line loop enters the opening, turn around and rotate the
rod hand so that the thumb is now in the normal position to
make a conventional forward cast.

ILLUSTRATION 110 — Continue forward and make your second forward cast, a conventional forward cast to your target
in front of you.

110

THE HIGH-FORWARD CAST

ILLUSTRATION 111 — When a higher than normal cast needs to be made, it is to the caster's advantage to begin with a back cast as low as possible. As we have learned, this is because

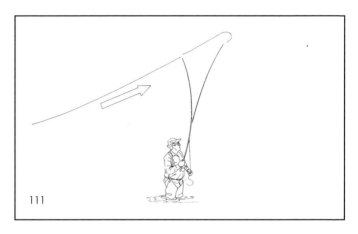

111

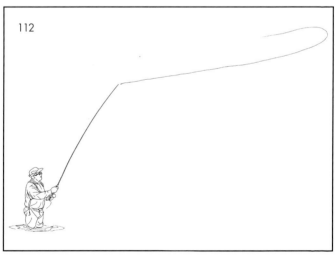

112

the more the rod and line travel in a straight direction to the target, the better is directed the energy of the cast. Here the angler has started with a very low back cast and a speed-up-and-stop has occurred at an upward angle.

ILLUSTRATION 112 — His forward cast will travel straight and high, wasting little energy.

THE LONG-LINE PICK-UP

Most average casters have to make several false casts to reach their target. But one of the most important techniques to master to progress to the advanced skill level in fly casting is the long-line pick-up. *The long-line pick-up is invaluable in many fly-fishing situations.* Of course, its principal value is that it will allow you to make some of your longest casts.

For a long cast, you need to extend and hold more line in the air outside the rod tip. The long-line pick-up does that. It allows you to place more line in the air, which, in turn, means that your fly will be closer to the target, and the amount of line you will have to shoot through the guides to reach the target on your final cast is considerably reduced.

And remember, *there is simply no better way to load a rod than to begin a back cast with the line on the water.* So if you can put a substantial portion of line on the water and then make a back cast, you can *really* load the rod, making possible some of the longest casts you'll ever be able to make.

The long-line pick-up can pay off in big dividends in typical fishing situations we all frequently encounter. For example, after you have made a cast and begun a retrieve, you suddenly see a fish rising well away from your fly (on a trout stream); or you see that your target fish is changing course (in saltwater). In either case, if you can pick up a long line, you can execute a new cast and quickly drop the fly near your desired target. If you can't pick up a long line, then you are forced to retrieve a lot of line before you can make your back cast, which consumes valuable time during which your fish may swim out of range.

On the long-line pick-up, the back cast should never be made until all the line *(not including the leader) has been lifted from the water.* The major reason why people cannot make a long-line pick-up is that *they leave a substantial amount of line on the surface of the water, where it is gripped so strongly by surface tension that they do not have the power to rip it loose.* Once all the line is above the surface and only the leader and fly are in the water, the back cast becomes infinitely easier.

Picking up a long line requires a few changes to the basic casting routine. The following sequence of seven illustrations demonstrates the technique.

113

ILLUSTRATION 113 — Lower the rod tip until it touches the water in front of you. Reach out and remove all slack, and after all slack is removed, immediately grip the line right beside the stripping guide of the rod, as shown.

ILLUSTRATION 114 — Begin to raise the rod tip vertically. This will lift a considerable portion of the line from the water. *It is vital that your line hand stay within inches of the stripping guide as the rod tip lifts line from the water.*

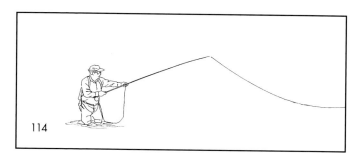

114

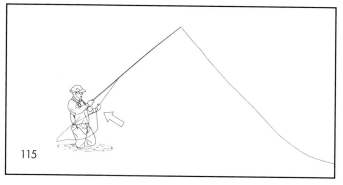

115

ILLUSTRATION 115 — It is at this point, when the rod has been raised, that a mistake is made by almost every fly fisherman when learning this cast. The inclination is to start drawing downward with the line hand as the rod tip is elevated. Resist this temptation! With the right technique, as shown, when the rod has been raised and as much line has been elevated off the water as possible, *the line hand should still be within inches of the stripping guide of the rod.*

ILLUSTRATION 116 — The line hand should remain as near as possible to the stripping guide as the rod continues to lift as much line from the surface as it can. As soon as you realize that the rod has lifted as much line as it can, begin a long, slow drawing downward motion with the line hand. This will

116

lift the remainder of the line from the water. But it is important to keep in mind that both motions — the lifting of the
rod and the drawing downward with the line hand, *should
not be done too slowly.* If either motion is too slow, the line
outside the rod tip as well as the line remaining just off the
surface will begin to sag and spoil the pick-up. The key here
is to lift the rod and draw down with the line hand just rapidly enough to keep the line from sagging, but not so fast as
to rip the line from the water.

ILLUSTRATION 117 — If things have been properly executed, at
this point your rod will be high, all line will be off the water,

117

and your rod hand will be almost straight up. Now, *make a back cast combined with a short and exceptionally fast single haul.* This is one cast for which the haul is essential. If all goes well, the line will flow effortlessly behind you.

ILLUSTRATION 118 — Because you have lifted an abnormally long length of line and thrown it behind you, you will need to pause just a little bit longer than you normally would before making a forward cast.

ILLUSTRATION 119 — Make a conventional forward cast, but aim it slightly higher than you would on a shorter cast. Any-

time you make a longer cast the line needs to be thrown at a slightly higher elevation, since it will be falling even as it progresses forward.

THE DOUBLE HAUL

As soon as an angler gains a little skill at fly casting the urge is to learn the double haul. But the double haul is not a panacea for fly casters. Unfortunately, many people learn the double haul before they should. In fact, some instructors teach the double haul within an hour or so of giving the first basic fly-casting lesson. I don't agree with that method, because while it's true that double hauling will help you throw a longer line, it can also mask or cover basic mistakes in rod-hand technique. Too many casters use the double haul not as a beneficial tool, *but as a way to throw their casting mistakes over a longer distance faster.*

I urge you to learn good rod-hand technique *before* you attempt the double haul. In the end, I promise you'll be a much better caster.

Having said that, I consider the double haul to be an exceedingly useful tool, which I use in *every* phase of my fly fishing. Every great fly caster uses it. If it is your goal to advance your casting skills to the highest levels of the game, you must master the double haul.

So what is a haul? A haul is a downward pull with the hand on the fly line, made during the speed-up-and-stop motions of a back or forward cast. Of course, a double haul is simply two single hauls working together on the same cast: the first single haul is made on the back cast; the second single haul is made on the forward cast.

By this time I'll bet you're sick and tired of reading what I'm going to say now. But it's so critical to good fly-casting technique that I'm going to risk your displeasure and say it again: *the shorter the distance the rod tip moves at the end of the cast, and the faster it moves over that short distance, coupled with an abrupt stop, the farther the line will travel.*

There are two factors involved in making the rod tip go faster and the line go farther: 1) *the speed* with which your rod hand accelerates the tip during the very last portion of the cast; and 2) *the distance* the rod tip moves during the speed-up-and-stop stroke. This rod tip distance is, of course, dictated by the distance the rod hand has moved on the haul.

A short haul makes the rod tip go faster. It is important, too, to realize that as long as you are hauling on the line, you are forcing the rod tip to flex. That means that if you want to make the line travel farther, you will need to make your hauls short and fast, as well as make sure that your line hand stops hauling at exactly the same time that your rod hand stops the tip's movement at the end of the cast.

You can demonstrate this for yourself. Put some line out-side the rod tip. Hold the rod vertically and look at the tip. Now, give a sharp downward jerk with the line hand. You will see the tip quickly accelerate. You will also notice that the longer the haul, the greater the arc the rod tip will travel through during the haul.

Another factor that needs to be remembered is that a fly line reaches the target by unrolling towards it. When a fly line has completely unrolled, *all forward motion ceases and the line begins falling*. As the haul is making the rod tip go faster, it is also making the line and fly travel a greater distance before the line completes its unrolling process. Thus, *the double haul works to translate increased rod tip speed into greater distance on the cast.*

OVERLEAF: *Joe Burke casts to fall browns on Utah's Green River, below Flaming Gorge Dam.*

120

Double Hauling Correctly

Here is a sequence of illustrations that demonstrates how to double haul correctly.

ILLUSTRATION 120 — The cast begins like any conventional one. The rod is lowered in preparation for making a back cast. All slack is removed from the line and the rod tip is then raised. For the most efficient double-hauling process, the *line hand should follow the reel (or chase it) as it is raised and should stay within 12 to 14 inches of the reel at all times.*

The illustration shows the angler's position just before the first single haul is going to be made on the back cast. Note that his line hand is close to the reel and there is no slack in the line between the stripping guide and the line hand. Also note that just before the haul is made the line hand is about even with the chin. This exact position is not necessary. But, as you study the next few illustrations, you will see at the completion of the haul, the line hand will end up being only a few inches lower than its initial starting position. In other words, *the haul moves a very short distance.*

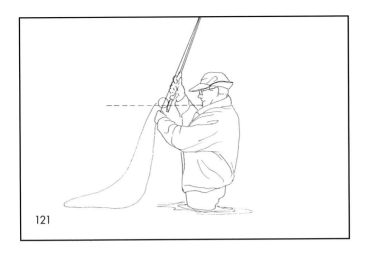

ILLUSTRATION 121 — Here is the most important factor in performing a superb haul. *The haul begins when the speed-up starts, and ends when the stop occurs. In other words, both the rod and the hauling hands begin and end their speed-up-and-stop at the same time.*

If the haul begins before the speed-up-and-stop, energy is wasted and the back cast loop will be more open. Remember Principle Number Four: the size of the loop is determined by the distance that the rod tip moves during the speed-up-and-stop. Because the haul causes the rod tip to flex, a long haul will cause the tip to flex a longer distance, with a loss of velocity, after the speed-up-and-stop on the back cast.

The same thing occurs on the forward cast and the single haul that accompanies it, but if it is done improperly, it creates even greater harm to the cast. A long haul causes the rod tip to flex over a greater distance (thus opening the loop), and so the quicker the rod stop at the completion of the speed-up-and-stop, the greater will be the line velocity being created. If you do not make simultaneous speed-ups-and-stops of the rod hand and the hauling hand, you will destroy line

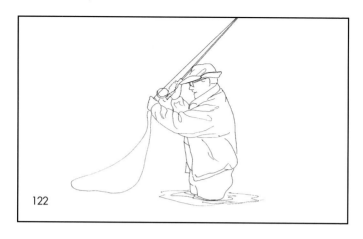

122

speed and fail to achieve the long distance cast you were after. You might say that with such incorrect hand technique,
your haul has been thrown out of sync. It is imperative that
the speed-up-and-stop for both the rod hand and the hauling
hand take place simultaneously.

ILLUSTRATION 122 — Begin the forward cast with both hands
close together as shown in the illustration.

123

ILLUSTRATION 123 — Begin the speed-up-and-stop of the rod and the forward haul at the same time, stopping both at the same time. This means the line hand hauls only a very short distance and stops abruptly. *A perfect haul means that the two working hands speed up and stop simultaneously.*

124

ILLUSTRATION 124 — The moment the rod stops the angler can shoot line to the target. Note that the line hand is still close to the reel at the stop.

Hauling When the Hands Are Apart

You will discover that there are certain fishing situations when your hands are well apart, yet you will still need to make a cast with a double haul. A typical situation is when you are stripping a lot of slack from the line, and you spy a fish moving away quickly, and a back cast needs to be made — immediately! At this moment your line hand could be well away from the reel. No problem. The essential key here is to realize that whatever their positions in relation to each other, the line and rod hands must start and stop at the same time during the speed-up-and-stop motion.

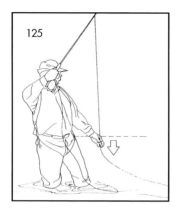 

ILLUSTRATION 125 — Here the angler has stripped in line and now has to make the back cast. Note that the line hand is at the top of the hip boot.

ILLUSTRATION 126 — He simply starts the line hand moving as the rod hand begins the first phase of the speed-up-and-stop — and stops the hauling motion when the rod hand stops. In this case, the line hand has actually moved just two or three inches and has stopped just below the boot top.

Double Hauling Incorrectly

You see it all the time. A fly fisherman is double hauling to get more distance. Down goes the line hand in a long, hard pulling of the line. He rips his underwear apart and his line hand ends up well below the knee. The rod hand rises a long way, and the rod sweeps forward, and again the line hand makes another l-o-n-g haul. Many times the fisherman looks like a chimpanzee hoeing potatoes. There is no question that this method of double hauling is hard work — and it shows. Worse, it is very inefficient.

Then, you see someone like Jim Green, the great fly caster and designer of so many Fenwick rods, who is one of the best double haulers I know. Jim's two hands rise together, there is an imperceptible swift hauling motion and the line hand barely seems to move. Then the rod comes forward and the line hand again barely moves — but the line shoots out a great distance. Jim's movements seem effortless, yet that fly streaks across the water. That is good double hauling.

The next two illustrations will show you bad double hauling technique.

ILLUSTRATION 127 — The line hand begins dragging downward as soon as the rod tip begins to move upward and continues moving downward long after the rod tip has stopped.

ILLUSTRATION 128 — When the forward cast begins, the angler must again haul on the line. The line hand that dove so far down on the back cast now has to rise to get ready for the second haul. This upward motion of the line hand places a great deal of slack in the line. If the back cast has been fast enough, it can help get rid of the slack, but this may affect the back cast's efficiency. Usually, the slack line has to be removed with forward rod motion. Remember Principle Number Two: you must get the end of the fly line moving before you can

127

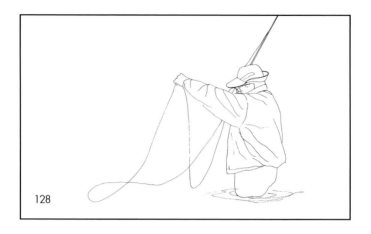

128

make the cast. Any forward rod motion that's wasted in re-moving the accumulated slack means less energy that can be deployed in making the forward cast.

To summarize double hauling:

1) *The speed-up-and-stop of the rod and the haul should start and stop at the same time.*

2) *The closer the two hands are together when double hauling the less likely for slack to occur in the line.*

There is one last and very important point that I have never seen in anything I've read about double hauling. You know that the faster that you move the rod tip during the speed-up-and-stop, the farther the cast will go. But, *almost all double haulers make their hauls at the same speed for every cast.*

If double hauling is already a part of your casting technique, think about this. You probably make all hauls at the same speed. What you need to realize is that the faster you make the haul (providing it is started and completed during the same period of the speed-up-and-stop), the faster the rod tip will travel and the more distance will be created on the cast. Thus, on a short cast where you don't need a lot of line speed, the double haul can be relatively slow. But when you really need to obtain great distance or throw into a strong wind, accelerate the double hauls much faster and you'll get a better cast.

CURVE CASTS

There are many fishing situations where a curve cast can be used to advantage. For example, a bass is lurking behind a stump and you would like to drop the fly behind the stump (perhaps even out of sight). Or, you may want to throw your fly so that the leader curves and drops the fly under a boat dock or an overhanging bush. One of the best assets of the curve cast is that it will permit you to make these kinds of casts and fish a streambank more effectively.

With conventional technique, a cast is made toward the bank at an angle and then the fly is retrieved. From the perspective of the fish, this type presentation presents a very slim silhouette: it is looking from the back to the front of the fly, much as you would view a knife from the point to the handle.

But since the curve cast propels the leader and part of the line in a curve, the fly, leader, and front of the line drop to the surface, parallel to the bank, permitting you to retrieve the fly *along* the bank, not away from it. This keeps the fly closer to cover for a longer period of time, and also gives the fish a much larger — and better to eat! — side view of the fly.

This same cast can be used when a fish lies close to you, facing either away or looking in your direction. A curve cast allows the fish to examine the fly on the retrieve for a considerable distance as the fly crosses in front of it. Whereas, for a fish facing away from you, the retrieve after a conventional cast causes the fly to move toward the fish in an attack position, from which the fish will shy away, as that is surely not the behavior of a natural food. Or, if the fish is facing you at a close distance and a conventional cast is made, the retrieve will draw the fish toward you, where it will likely see you and spook. The curve cast will eliminate such problems.

There are two types of curve casts, vertical and side. Let's examine the side curve cast first. It's an easy cast to master.

The Side Curve Cast

ILLUSTRATION 129 — Here's a mental exercise that may help you to set yourself up to make an accurate side curve cast. Imagine that you are the angler in the illustration, pointing at the target with your rod hand, and pointing 90 degrees to your side with your other hand. Visualize that on your back cast, keeping the rod low and parallel to the surface of the water, you are going to sweep your rod along the curve that is describing that 90-degree angle.

ILLUSTRATION 130 — So let's initiate that low back cast. *And remember, a low back cast is vital to success.* If a high back cast is made, then the rod will be forced to travel in a downward direction on the forward cast as it moves toward the target, which is *not* what you want to do. *I can't emphasize enough*

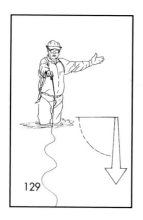

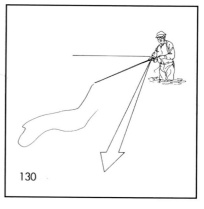

that you must make a low back cast and then bring the rod forward on a plane that is parallel to the surface during the entire forward cast. Now, when the rod tip is at a 45-degree angle from the target, make a hard, fast speed-up-and-stop. This will produce a good side curve cast. A major reason for anglers not mastering this simple cast is that they bring their rod forward at a downward angle and don't come to a dead stop.

ILLUSTRATION 131 — One of the keys to making a successful side curve cast is how quickly (or how hard) you stop the rod tip when it is 45 degrees from the target. Remember, the fly line and leader are going to go in the direction in which the rod tip stops. When you carry the rod forward and sideways and parallel to the surface and stop, the rod tip will curve to the left — causing the leader and line end to follow the same curved path, as shown. The quicker you make the speed-up-and-stop the more the tip curves on that stop. And, the more the tip curves, the larger will be the resulting curve at the end of the cast. If you know how to double haul, make a very fast haul at the end of the cast (during the speed-up-and-stop). This will increase the size of the curve thrown in the leader and line end.

131

The Vertical Curve Cast

The side curve cast has the inherent weakness (unless you are ambidextrous) that it can only be made on one side of the angler (which may not be where the fish are). It also requires a fair amount of open space.

However, the vertical curve cast can be used to make curves to the left or right of the angler and as close as 10 feet or as far away as 70 feet, and requires only a minimal amount of overhead space for the rod to travel in. Therefore, it is much more versatile and can be used in many more fishing situations than the side curve cast. But it is a much more difficult cast to execute properly. *In fact, it is the most difficult of all casts I try to teach students.* However, once mastered, it can be one of the most useful tools in your fishing arsenal.

I urge you to learn this cast. Pay very close attention to the following illustrations and instructions (which assume the caster is right-handed) which demonstrate executing the cast correctly to the left and right sides of the angler. Also, as a teaching device, I've included a couple of illustrations that show how to throw this cast the wrong way.

132

ILLUSTRATION 132 *(Vertical Curve Cast to the Left)* — A conventional back cast has been made, and the rod is being brought forward to the position where the speed-up-and-stop is to be made.

ILLUSTRATION 133 *(Vertical Curve Cast to the Left)* — Remember, the line and fly are going to go in the direction in which the rod tip stops. What you want to do here — *during the speed-up-and-stop* — is to make the rod travel to the left in a very swift, short, horizontal arc. *Note that the rod hand has traveled in a level horizontal plane.* In other words, if you have executed this hand movement correctly, if at the initiation of the forward cast your rod hand was, say, 4 feet and 2 inches above the water, at the completion of the speed-up-and-stop motion (accompanied by the horizontal swing of your rod hand to the left), the cast should end with your rod hand still exactly 4 feet and 2 inches above the surface.

This bears repeating: *the rod hand has to travel in a horizontal arc.* Of course, if your rod hand makes a very long sweep around the arc, just as in any other cast, you will produce a

133

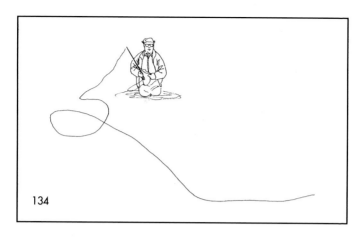

134

large loop. Most of the time, you'll want to make your hand swing and speed-up-and-stop fast and short — just as you would with any other good cast.

Upon completion of the speed-up-and-stop, the rod tip will continue downward toward the surface of the water into a normal fishing position.

ILLUSTRATION 134 (*Vertical Curve Cast to the Left*) — If you have swept the rod hand to the left in a horizontal plane as you were simultaneously executing your speed-up-and-stop, as your forward cast is completed you will throw a nice curve to the left, as shown.

Also, if you have properly executed the vertical curve cast, you will throw a curve *in the direction you are facing*. Therefore, if you want to throw a curve around a target positioned at an angle of, say, 45 degrees from you, simply rotate your body 45 degrees until you face the target, make a vertical curve cast, and your line, leader, and fly will curve around the target.

Now, as a further aid to instruction, here are two illustrations that I hope will demonstrate why most people do not master the vertical curve cast.

135

ILLUSTRATION 135 *(Vertical Curve Cast to the Left — Wrong Way)*
— Note in this illustration that as the speed-up-and-stop
begins, the rod tip is being tilted, *the rod is no longer in a vertical position,* and *the rod hand is beginning to move downward
as it travels to the left.* Compare this to Illustration 133 on page
129, in which, during the travel motion of the speed-up-and-
stop, while the rod hand was making its horizontal sweep, it
remained on the same level plane, *holding the rod in a vertical
position.* This is a critical observation.

What is vital to understand is that you cannot throw a
proper vertical curve cast *unless the hand travels in a horizontal plane during the speed-up-and-stop,* and the horizontal plane
is destroyed when the rod hand begins to move downward.

ILLUSTRATION 136 *(Vertical Curve Cast to the Left — Wrong Way)*
— As the rod continues to sweep downward and ends as
shown, no curve cast will result. The reason is this: the fly is
going to go in the direction in which the rod tip traveled during the speed-up-and-stop. If you do not cause the rod hand
to travel to the left in a horizontal plane, but instead, sweep it
to the left and down, you will throw the line in the water in

136

front of you before the line ever has a chance to complete the curve. *This is the major reason why many people cannot master a vertical curve cast.*

But, there is also another reason people fail on this cast. If you make the speed-up-and-stop going straight ahead, *but delay in moving the rod hand on its horizontal swing* until after the speed-up-and-stop motion is over, *no curve will result.*

Remember the example I gave earlier in the book about pulling the trigger on a rifle and then throwing the rifle down — illustrating the point that after the bullet has been fired and is on its way to the target, you can no longer influence its flight path? The same principle applies here. If you make the speed-up-and-stop (fire the bullet from the rifle) and then try to make a curve in the line (throw the rifle down), you will get the same result. When you made your speed-up-and-stop going straight ahead, the direction of the line was then fixed to travel straight ahead, and you can no longer influence its direction.

Because of the anatomical structure of the arm, a right-hander cannot easily move his right arm in a horizontal plane when trying to throw a vertical curve cast to the right (or a left-hander trying to throw to the left). *But it is vital during the speed-up-and-stop that the rod tip still travel in a horizontal plane, parallel to the water's surface.* To overcome this anatomical handicap it will be necessary to tilt the rod forward, so you can make the proper stroke.

137

ILLUSTRATION 137 (*Vertical Curve Cast to the Right*) — Just before the speed-up-and-stop, the rod hand is carried well in front of the body, as shown. Note that the rod hand is as high as the head and the rod tip is tilted forward and to the side. This attitude of the rod will permit you to make a horizontal speed-up-and-stop stroke to the right.

ILLUSTRATION 138 (*Vertical Curve Cast to the Right*) — Be very careful to carry the speed-up-and-stop at the same height from the surface of the water (just as you did when making a curve to the left), maintaining the stroke on the same plane, or horizontal to the surface.

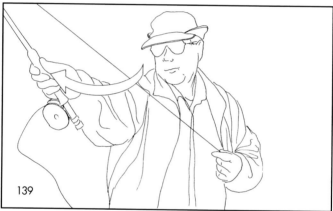

ILLUSTRATION 139 (*Vertical Curve Cast to the Right*) — At the end of the stroke the knuckles of the rod hand should be positioned at right angles to the body, as shown.

ILLUSTRATION 140 (*Vertical Curve Cast to the Right*) — If the rod hand was swept parallel to the water during the speed-up-and-stop motion, ending as shown in Illustration 139, you will throw a curve to the right, as shown.

140

THE TUCK CAST

The tuck cast is extremely useful for anglers who fish in current and are offering underwater flies to fish. This cast causes the leader and line to "tuck" back under the forward portion of the fly line. The fly begins to sink upon contact with the water as the slack placed in the cast drifts downstream. The result is that the fly can sink deeper than one that was cast on a straight line. It is generally regarded as a technique to be used for nymph fishing. But anytime you want the fly to drift naturally and deeper in the current, it will work with any type of subsurface fly.

Almost everyone familiar with the tuck cast regards it also as a method of tucking the leader and fly *directly underneath* the line as it falls to the water. But, the cast can be modified so that curves to the right or left are easily obtained. You'll find that the curve tuck cast will often catch more fish than one cast in a vertical plane.

OVERLEAF: *Lefty Kreh executes a forward cast on Big Spring in south central Pennsylvania.*

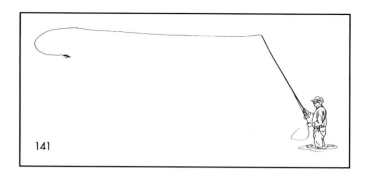

141

ILLUSTRATION 141 — A high vertical cast is made, as shown in the illustration. *The important factor here is that the line should obtain a very high amount of speed. Enough speed should be developed to make a cast that would travel two or three times farther than would normally be used for the amount of line being cast. Without excessive speed the tuck cast won't work!* It also helps on the forward cast to use a single haul to obtain greater line speed.

The rod is stopped *at a near vertical position.* The more vertically the rod is stopped (combined with the greater line speed) the more of the leader and fly will tuck on the cast. *The lower the elevation of the rod on the forward stop, the less tuck can occur.* The rod needs to be stopped dead at the end of the cast. And it is vital to hold the rod *motionless* until after the tuck occurs. Any backward or forward rod movement will detract from the amount of leader that is tucked under. *Creating excessive line speed on the forward cast and maintaining a stationary rod position are the two most important factors in making a good tuck cast.*

ILLUSTRATION 142 — If the rod is held perfectly motionless at the vertical angle shown in the illustration, the force of the speedy forward cast will straighten the line and bend the rod. Then, the rod tip will recoil. If the rod is held motionless, *it is*

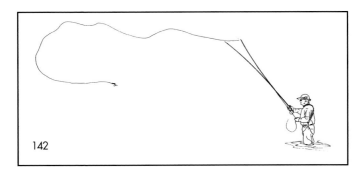

142

the recoiling of the rod tip that creates the tuck. The rod jolting backwards will jerk the line to the rear and cause the leader and forward portion of the line to tuck under the forward portion of the line.

ILLUSTRATION 143 — The line begins falling to the water with the leader and some of the forward portion of the line tucked back under. The rod tip is dropped as the line begins to fall to the water. And, the line touches down with the leader and some of the front portion of the fly line tucked well back under the balance of the fly line. The more tuck desired, the greater the line speed that should be created on the forward cast. The fly begins to sink as the line begins drifting downstream. Because of the slack, the fly is able to dive deeper before the retrieve begins.

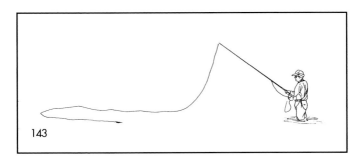

143

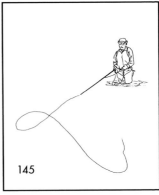

144

145

ILLUSTRATION 144 (*Tuck Cast with Curve to the Left*) — The tuck cast can be made so that the line tucks with a curve to the left or right of the angler. This is very advantageous in many fishing situations. For example, if you are wading upstream with the streambank on your left, and you need to get a nymph or streamer close to the bank and deeper in the water for the downstream drift, use the tuck cast with curve to the left. Make a conventional tuck cast as already explained with one exception — tilt the rod to the right of the shoulder.

146

147

ILLUSTRATION 145 (*Tuck Cast with Curve to the Left*) — Follow all conventional tuck cast procedures and the rod tilted to the right will cause the leader and fly to tuck to the left.

ILLUSTRATION 146 (*Tuck Cast with Curve to the Right*) — If you would like to make a tuck cast that causes the leader and fly to curve under and to the right, simply tilt the rod to the left of your shoulder.

ILLUSTRATION 147 (*Tuck Cast with Curve to the Right*) — If the rod is held tilted to the left and all tuck cast procedures are followed, the leader and fly will nicely tuck back under in a curve to the right.

THE SLACK LINE CAST

When fishing in a stream, most dry-fly presentations are made upstream. But whether you are fishing upstream or downstream, with all dry-fly presentations it is imperative that the leader, and hopefully, the forward portion of the fly line, fall to the surface in soft curls or waves. If the line and leader fall to the water in a straight line, the current will pull against the leader, causing the fly to drag unnaturally and produce a poor presentation to the fish.

Many dry-fly fishermen have a problem creating these soft waves after the cast. Actually, the problem is pretty simple to solve. The following illustrations, which depict a typical upstream presentation, explain why some people can't get those soft waves, and how to correct the situation.

ILLUSTRATION 148 — This upstream cast has started just fine, at a high elevation. (You should go even higher on a downstream presentation, if possible.) When its energy is exhausted

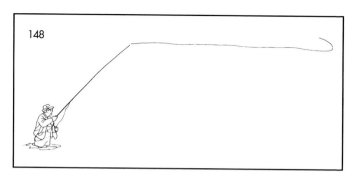

148

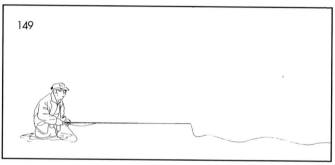

149

and the cast is ending, immediate action needs to be taken to place the line on the surface of the water in soft waves.

ILLUSTRATION 149 — The instant the fly line and leader are fully extended (the total forward cast is finished), drop the arm and the rod as shown. You will find that numerous and desirable soft waves have been created in the forward portion of the line and the leader.

ILLUSTRATION 150 — But, if the rod remains elevated for even a few seconds, as shown, few, if any, waves will be created in the line.

ILLUSTRATION 151 — What happens is this. The line from the

150

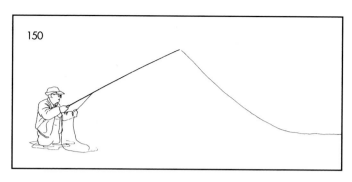

151

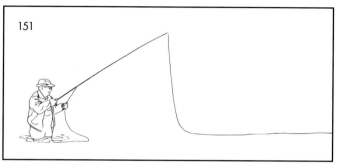

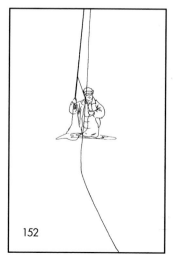

152

153

143

rod tip to the surface begins to sag. As it does, it drifts back toward the angler, pulling out any accumulated waves, which results in the line falling straight.

ILLUSTRATION 152 — At the end of the cast, if the rod remains elevated for even a short time, the sag will pull the line straight, as shown.

ILLUSTRATION 153 — But, if the rod is dropped immediately, those soft waves will be created.

THE SKIP CAST

This is one of the oldest casts I know. I learned it early in my fly-fishing career. Many years ago I fished the Potomac River for smallmouth bass. There were huge numbers of silver maple trees that grew along the shores of the river. Many of their limbs hung low over the water, forming a shady shelter for the smallmouths that would hide there. With a conventional cast, you simply couldn't get the fly way back under those overhanging limbs.

One day I remembered how I used to skip small flat rocks across the surface of the water. I began experimenting and taught myself how to make a fly line skip in the same manner, so that it could carry the fly way back into those shadows. I caught a lot of bass using this cast. I was even a bit puffed up about how I had "developed" a special new fly cast. Of course, later I learned that the skip cast had been around a long, long time.

It is a terrific cast to drive popping bugs and flies back under boat docks. I often use it to deliver a dry fly to a fish holding in a difficult position. It's also great for getting a nymph or streamer to a wary fish. It is very helpful, too, when you want

144

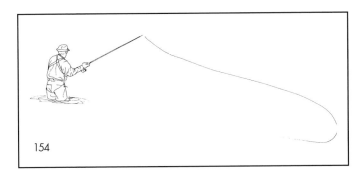

154

to drive a fly back under the mangrove branches to seek out snook, tarpon, and redfish. In fact, there is almost no fishing situation I can think of where a skip cast won't come in handy.

ILLUSTRATION 154 — Face your target and make a low side cast. *You cannot make a skip cast if you make an elevated back cast.* The line on the back cast should travel *low and parallel with the water* — a vital point.

ILLUSTRATION 155 — Bring the rod sweeping forward in a side cast with the tip close to and parallel with the surface. Aside from the need to make a low side cast to the front, you need to do two additional things to make a good skip cast:

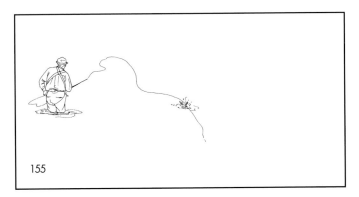

155

1) You must generate a little more than normal line speed on the forward cast. The reason for this is that the fly and a portion of the leader and perhaps the front of the line are going to contact the water for the skip. This contact will slow the forward cast, so a bit of additional line speed is needed. If you know how to haul, a strong haul on the forward cast helps.

2) As you are coming forward with the cast, you need to have the front portion of the fly line make contact with the water either slightly behind or even with your body. When you were young and threw a stone to make it skip, you didn't throw it so it hit the water near the target. Instead, you aimed the stone to strike the surface just in front of you, and then it made one or more skips as it skittered across the surface.

ILLUSTRATION 156 — If you have generated enough line speed and you contacted the water at the right place, the fly will skip low to the surface and travel to the target.

THE SHORT CAST

You'll find that there will be times when you will be faced with making a very short cast, with only the leader and just a little bit of fly line outside your rod tip. This happens frequently in dry-fly or nymph fishing — particularly in windy conditions that may hinder a long cast — and often in saltwater when you need to make a quick cast to a bonefish or barracuda that has swum quite close to your boat without being aware of your presence.

A good short cast is by no means an easy cast for most people. For one thing, very few people ever practice the short cast. But what makes the cast difficult is that you don't have enough line weight outside the rod tip to load the rod properly so that the leader can unroll for a decent presentation of the fly.

When a very short cast is required, you will need to use a specialized casting technique. Rules are made to be broken, and while the five basic principles of the casting method I advocate apply to all casting situations, I recognize that for the short cast, we're going to have to improvise and bend the rules a bit. The next sequence of illustrations demonstrates how the short cast should be made.

ILLUSTRATION 157 — With a long leader and only a few feet of line outside the guides, you need to lower the rod until the tip is almost in the water.

ILLUSTRATION 158 — The rod is brought upward at a near-vertical angle with smooth acceleration until the rod hand is well

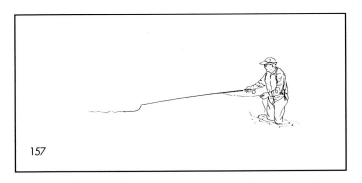

157

158

above the head. Then your speed-up-and-stop on the back cast should be made as quickly and as briefly as you can make it. The stop is directed only slightly to the rear and almost overhead. To direct the cast properly, imagine that you are standing below and about 10 feet in front of a balcony. What you are attempting to do is throw the cast so that it is directed at the balcony — or almost straight upward.

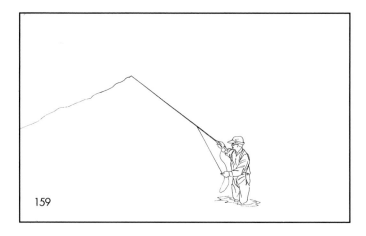

159

ILLUSTRATION 159 — Almost as soon as the stop on the back cast is made, the forward cast should begin. And, the forward acceleration of the rod prior to the speed-up-and-stop should be short, perhaps only six inches to a foot. Then a speed-up-and-stop is made so that the rod tip *is directed at an elevation just slightly higher than the target.*

On a conventional cast at a greater distance, when you have some line weight outside the rod tip assisting the cast, you normally would direct your fly at a considerable elevation above the target, allowing the leader to unroll and fall gently onto the surface of the water. But with so little line outside the rod tip on the short cast, there's just not enough energy created in the cast to turn the leader over properly, so you need to get the fly closer to the target as quickly as you can to use whatever line energy you do have.

However, this certainly does not mean that you should throw the cast directly at the target. The reason being as in all casts, the fly will likely splash heavily onto the surface and frighten the fish.

With the short cast, what you are doing is literally throwing as high a back cast as you can, and then dragging the line forward and downward. There are several keys to this cast which sort of violate good casting principles, but since so little line is being cast, the technique works.

To summarize the steps for making the short cast:

1) Starting with a low rod, you need to make a long acceleration and a speed-up-and-stop that ends with the hand high above the head;

2) The back cast is directed almost vertically to the rear;

3) On the forward cast the rod hand moves only a very short distance before the speed-up-and-stop occurs, and the speed-up-and-stop is directed straight ahead at the target at a lower than normal elevation.

Most of the time the angler will want to make a small, tight loop, which directs most of the caster's energy at the target. But there are some situations when the ability to throw a large loop is a decided advantage.

One such situation occurs frequently with trout fishermen who have added split-shot, or a heavy strike indicator, or one or more dropper flies, to a long, light leader and tippet.

With a leader weighted down with such items, when a conventional cast is made with a fairly tight loop, at the end of the back cast *the direction of the cast will change abruptly*. This is what causes messy tangles. The leader and all the items attached to it are going back and away from the caster, and as the forward cast is made, the sudden change in direction of the fly line jerks on the leader, causing it to run into itself and create elaborate monofilament birds' nests and horrendous tangles.

This same problem occurs when an angler is using a heavy fly that is out of balance with the weight of his leader. For example, a trout fisherman using a 5X leader who clips off a dry fly and, to save time without changing to a heavy leader, attaches a heavily weighted nymph to his original very light leader. Or it could be a saltwater fly fisherman who exchanges a small bonefish fly for a heavy permit crab pattern. With such heavy terminals on light leaders, when a fast, tight loop is driven backward and the direction changed abruptly, there will be a sudden jerk on the leader that either causes the fragile tippet to break or snap back and tangle in the leader. In these situations, what is needed is a large-loop cast that will permit you to change casting directions, from the back to the forward cast, *slowly enough to avoid creating such jolts* in the leader.

This same technique can be used to great advantage when you need to make a relatively long cast in front, but you have a wall or obstruction not too far behind you. A large unrolling back-cast loop will keep the line moving, and yet not permit it to travel in a straight line, which would mean throwing the line into the obstruction.

As you fish, you will find a number of such situations where the ability to throw a larger loop is desirable. Remember, the size of the loop is determined by the distance that the rod tip travels during the speed-up-and-stop portion of the cast. It follows that if you *simply increase the length of the speed-up-and-stop, you will increase loop size.* Let's illustrate this:

ILLUSTRATION 160 — The rod is lowered so that the tip is nearly in the water. All slack is removed and the rod is lifted to get the line end moving and out of the water. A long speed-up-and-stop is made. Be sure that the rod tip stops at some upward direction or you will throw the fly down in the water behind you. Note in the illustration that the rod tip is well behind the angler. You must get the rod well back on such a cast so that as you commence the forward cast you can make a long drawing-forward motion to keep the loop open and the leader taut to draw any slack from the line.

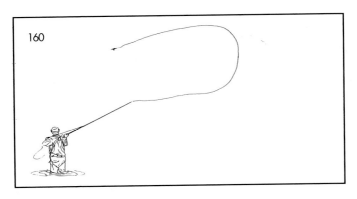

160

OVERLEAF: *Ed Jaworowski on the Potomac River in Maryland.*

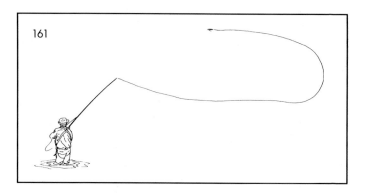

161

ILLUSTRATION 161 — The rod is drawn *s-l-o-w-l-y* forward, which will cause the leader and fly to travel around a wide circle behind you as the back cast is completed and the forward cast begins. This wide circling motion keeps the leader taut and all heavy attachments on the line separated and under control.

TIGHT-LOOP EXERCISE #1 (USE OF THE HULA HOOP FOR LOOP CONTROL PRACTICE)

The size of the loop you cast is dependent upon how long the distance is that the rod tip moves during the final speed-up-and-stop at the very end of the cast. There is a long gradual acceleration — then a final speed-up-and-stop to form the loop and direct the cast. Almost all casters move the rod through too long a distance on the speed-up-and-stop, creating too big a loop, a poor one.

The major reason most people make too big a loop is they don't understand (or just forget, for it's really a very simple principle) the physics of using a long flexible lever (rod) that is usually 8 1/2 feet or longer! They insist upon equating how much movement they make at the butt of the rod with the movement that is being made at the other end of the lever. Remember, it is the distance that *the rod tip moves* during the speed-up-and-stop that is critical to good casting technique. A tiny back and forth motion of the rod hand will only move the butt of rod slightly. But that tiny movement is greatly magnified at the rod tip. To demonstrate this, hold the rod parallel to the ground. Now, rock the rod hand back and forth a few inches, and you will instantly see that the tip is swaying *several feet*.

When I am trying to teach casters how to make a tighter loop, I often say to them, "You can't make the hand motion during the speed-up-and-stop too short."

Fortunately, there is a simple device that will help you gain loop control — a hula hoop.

ILLUSTRATION 162 — Suspend a hula hoop in a stable position so that the bottom of the ring is about even with the top of your head.

Then begin by standing back about 20 feet and try to cast a tight loop through the hula hoop. If you are a fairly experi-

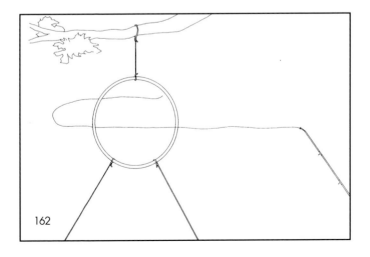

162

enced fly caster, you'll be able to do that. Continue casting, backing away from the hoop until you find that most of your casts won't travel through the hoop. Stay at that distance until you can repeatedly throw your loop through the hoop. Then step back even more.

Too big a loop will strike the facing edge of the hula hoop and not travel through. With this sort of trial-and-error practice, you should be able to condition and imprint on your mind and casting muscles this essential principle that the shorter the distance you move the rod tip during the speed-up-and-stop at the end of the cast, the tighter will be your loop. When you finally learn to control the distance of the speed-up-and-stop, you should be able to throw at least 70 feet of fly line through the hoop.

TIGHT-LOOP EXERCISE #2 (THROWING THE FLY LINE AT THE ROD TIP)

Here is another exercise I have devised that has produced remarkable results with people who are already a fair hand at fly casting. I have had many anglers who could learn to throw maybe 70 feet of fly line with a very tight loop after making just a few casts with this exercise.

ILLUSTRATION 163 — With the fly line on the surface of the water and ready for the back cast, play a mental game with yourself. Say confidently to yourself, "When I make this back cast, I am going to try to throw the line so that it will strike against the tip of the rod." In other words, you want the line to crash into the rod tip.

The same procedure is used on the forward cast. During the speed-up-and-stop motion, try to concentrate on throwing the line so it will actually hit the rod tip.

163

You'll find that it is actually quite difficult to strike the rod tip with the fly line. But, for many of my students, I have found that this exercise is very useful in that it forces them to stop their rod tip in the direction they want their fly line to travel, which works to shorten their speed-up-and-stop stroke and tightens their loop.

INDEX